JAZZ GUITA IMPROVISATION STRATEGIES

STEVEN KIRBY

BERKLEE PRESS

Editor in Chief: Jonathan Feist
Senior Vice President of Online Learning and Continuing Education/CEO of Berklee Online: Debbie Cavalier
Vice President of Enrollment Marketing and Management: Mike King
Vice President of Academic Strategy: Carin Nuernberg
Editorial Assistant: Brittany McCorriston

ISBN 978-0-87639-205-8

1140 Boylston Street
Boston, MA 02215-3693 USA
(617) 747-2146

Visit Berklee Press Online at
www.berkleepress.com

Study music online at
online.berklee.edu

DISTRIBUTED BY

HAL•LEONARD®
7777 W. BLUEMOUND RD. P.O. BOX 13819
MILWAUKEE, WISCONSIN 53213

Visit Hal Leonard Online
www.halleonard.com

Berklee Press, a publishing activity of Berklee College of Music, is a not-for-profit educational publisher.
Available proceeds from the sales of our products are contributed to the scholarship funds of the college.

CONTENTS

ACKNOWLEDGEMENTS

Thanks to my many wonderful colleagues in the playing, composing, and teaching realms who help me learn and grow each day. You are too numerous to list individually but are an inspiration every day. Thanks to Mike Connors (drums) and Mark Poniatowski (bass) for playing on the tracks, for your stellar musicianship, and great friendship. It's always such a pleasure working with you both. Thank you to Martin Gioani (guitare-improvisation.com) for providing the backing track portion of audio for "Improvised 'Bird Blues' Solo with Rhythmic Variation" (track 64). To the many creative improvising musicians, both famous and obscure, who have inspired me to play, learn, and teach. This book, in a way, is for my sixteen-year-old self, and all aspiring musicians who are trying to figure out a way to get a handle on "playing over changes" on the guitar. Thanks to David Harris, Boy and Dog Studios (Methuen, MA), and Chillhouse Studio (Chelsea, MA) for recording the audio, and to Jonathan Feist and the team at Berklee Press who helped get the book across the finish line; your efforts are greatly appreciated.

This book is dedicated to my wife, Kristine, for her love, support, and musical sharing, and to our daughter Poornima, for her uplifting and generous spirit, creative work, and editing and writing skills.

A Pathway to "Making the Changes"

The ability to improvise fluently over changing harmony opens up an exhilarating array of creative expression. It also increases career options in the music industry. Mastering it is a learning task that can seem overwhelming, comparable to spontaneously composing well-constructed stories in a new language—all while adhering to a particular metric structure! Tackling this task on the guitar, with its asymmetrical tuning system and unique technical obstacles, presents guitarists with additional challenges.

As with learning a language, you improve faster if you listen to, and eventually converse with, people who already speak the language well. While this book will provide you with many useful strategies, the *primary, indispensable way* to learn to improvise is to do a lot of *deep listening, analysis, and focused practice for assimilation*. That is, carefully check out what sounds great, use analysis to understand why, and practice in a focused way to incorporate the inspiring and effective elements into your own playing.

As you immerse yourself in the language of jazz improvisation, you will gradually be able to follow the time-honored advice for learning any art form: *imitate, assimilate, innovate.*

This book will help you primarily with the "imitate and assimilate" portions of the task, and it can lay the foundation for innovation too. It should be used in tandem with an ongoing program of deep listening, active transcription, and analysis. You should always be in the process of learning music that inspires you.

The information in this book is presented in a practical way. When it comes to playing over changes, these strategies can take the aspiring improvising guitarist from non-functional to functional—from not being able to connect to the changing harmony to being able to "make the changes," because you will have a method that works.

The material in the book is connected to five strategies for developing your ability to improvise.

Strategy 1. Exploit simple techniques.

- In learning to improvise over changing harmony, prioritize learning a lot about a little, not a little about a lot. Less is more.

- Practice a select group of flexible/powerful techniques to the point of practical usefulness. The momentum from that success will inspire your continued learning.

Strategy 2. Break it down to build it up.

- Convert big practice tasks into small, achievable, short-term goals.

- *Design* your practice time. Avoid practicing mindlessly, without clear direction. Aim to achieve feelings of success multiple times in each practice session, working towards reaching short term goals.

Short term goals lead to long term success. By "short term," I mean a goal that you think you can *achieve in fifteen minutes or less.* This amount of time is based on established science about effective learning and the brain.

Short-term goal-setting has two components: the breaking down part and the measurement part. Measuring will be discussed in strategy 3.

Strategies for breaking down long-term goals down into small, short-term learning chunks include:

- Thinking in four-note cells (chapter 1). Later, other groupings can be used.

- Constant note-value soloing (chapter 1).

- Focusing on transition points between chord changes and scale changes (chapter 4).

- "Lick Looping" (chapter 5).

- Chord Pairing, dealing with only two chords at a time and eventually chaining those pairs into longer groups (chapters 5 and 6).

Strategy 3. Measure your progress.

Meaningful measuring makes mastery!

Mastery is the point at which you can perform a skill reliably and consistently. Measuring your progress will help you get to mastery.

Learn to measure your progress by the metrics of mastery. Set the bar high, but approach it gradually with focus and fun via strategy 2.

Tools for measuring your level of mastery include:

- Metronome, drum loops, backing tracks.

- Defining conditions/parameters (articulation, technique, tempo, number of repetitions).

Metrics of mastery:

- **Memory.** You can play the idea without referencing notation or a recording.

- **Technical control of articulation and tempo.** You can play the idea repeatedly (at least three times consecutively), cleanly, and reliably at a given steady tempo with a particular articulation.

- **Transposition.** You can transpose the idea to multiple different keys or over different harmonies in real time.

- **Note and fretboard knowledge.** You can play the idea or passage in different octaves and at the same pitch level in multiple locations on the guitar neck.

- **Ear training/inner hearing.** You can internally and externally sing the lines you are playing.

- **Ear to instrument.** You can "pre-hear" a musical idea and then play it on your instrument accurately and instantaneously.

- **Control of melody/harmony relationships.** You can improvise an effective constant-note value solo that reflects the underlying harmony of a given set of chord changes.

- **Control of an improvisational tool/concept.** You can improvise using the concept in tempo, in a musically effective way.

- **Full internalization of understanding.** You can explain and teach what you've learned to someone else.

Combining Strategies 2 and 3:

- Set a short-term goal (achievable in fifteen minutes or less).

- Decide how to measure your mastery of that goal (tempo, number of repetitions). For example, three accurate, flawlessly performed repetitions, in perfect tempo (without speeding up or slowing down).

Learning is incremental and often feels like you are taking three steps forward and two steps back. Everyone needs to review material many times during multiple practice sessions to reinforce newly learned material, but achieving a mastery metric at least indicates you are likely ready to add at least one, well chosen, new element of challenge. The new element might be:

- A small increase or decrease of tempo.

- Different fingering.

- Applying it to a different chord/key.

- Different articulation (picking, legato, etc.).

Strategy 4. Master the fretboard.

The guitar's structure can box you in. Learn to transcend its limitations with flexible fingering strategies (see chapter 5).

Flexible fingerings facilitate fluidity and freedom!

Strategy 5. Practice effectively.

To learn more, better, in less time, use short, focused, and frequent practice sessions. Avoid sporadic, unfocused, and infrequent sessions, even if they are longer.

The effectiveness of this strategy has been confirmed by scientific research about practice and learning. One readable and scientifically informed book on how to practice effectively is *The Talent Code* by Daniel Coyle.

Exactly how you implement your practicing content and session length needs to be customized and flexible. The important thing is to understand the importance of regulating your practice time for optimal effectiveness and to avoid injury. Research into the brain reveals that certain principles apply to everyone, but at the same time, each of us needs to use those principles in an individualized way.

One approach is "20/20/20":

- Practice for 20 minutes.

- Take a break and walk 20 paces.

- Breathe deeply for 20 seconds.

Refocus and repeat.

THE UNIVERSAL TO THE PARTICULAR

This book teaches core improvisation techniques, organizing them in a way that addresses the specific challenges encountered by guitarists.

What will you be able to do after reading and practicing with this book?

You'll be able to play over selected changing harmony with musical logic and growing confidence and creativity. I call this the ability to create "flow" through the changes.

The criteria for "flow."

All great improvisers connect their melodies with the underlying harmony. Their improvisations are melodic, but they also "describe" the harmony so well that if you remove the accompanying harmonic layer, you can still sense the chord changes.

Developing the ability to "flow" through the changes is a prerequisite to becoming a great improviser. On the path to this skill, we will use the practical application of proven melody/harmony and voice-leading guidelines demonstrated by musical giants as diverse as J. S. Bach, Charlie Parker, and John Coltrane.

Learning to play over changes does require significant amounts of practice time, but the creative fun and fulfillment will make the time feel well worth it. This book will help you steadily improve on your way toward achieving heightened musical freedom and expression in your improvising.

ABOUT THE AUDIO

To access the accompanying audio, go to www.halleonard.com/mylibrary and enter the code found on the first page of this book. This will grant you instant access to every example. Examples with accompanying audio are marked with an audio icon. These tracks are tuned to A440.

Start with track 1, which is an introduction.

Audio 1

CHAPTER 1

The "Flow"

"Flow" is the term I'm using to describe a series of characteristics in effective improvised melodies. Melodies with "flow" have note content that "describes" the underlying harmony while simultaneously including motivic development and an overall pleasing balance of vertical and horizontal movement. Learning to create a sense of "flow" within a melody that is built exclusively from a constant note value—that is, without any rhythmic variety—is an extremely effective way for improvisers to develop both melodic and harmonic mastery. Working on this skill ultimately helps in the creation of harmonically connected, rhythmically varied melodies, too.

In this chapter and throughout this book, we will look at some of the building blocks for creating a sense of flow in constant eighth-note melodies. The term "constant note value" in this book can apply to straight or swing performances ($\sqcap = \overset{3}{\sqcap}$), in eighth notes or sixteenth notes.

The building blocks for creating flow:

- Developing extended melodies out of four-note cells.
- Connecting chords through voice leading.
- Understand the functionality of notes.
- Using the relationships between scales and chords.

Listen to this solo chorus on a jazz blues (track 2) while looking at the chart in figure 1.1.

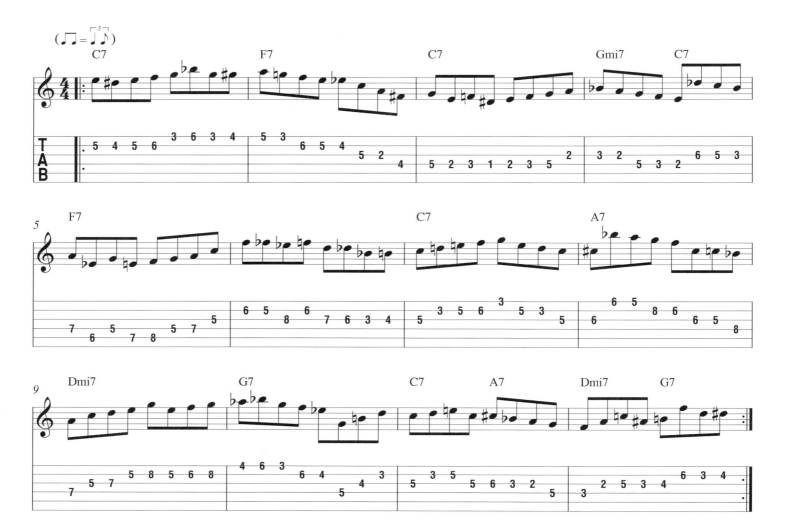

FIG. 1.1. Blues in C

Now, listen to the audio of the "melody only" version of this same solo (track 3). Can you still sense the melody's underlying harmony?

Even with the melody unsupported by chords, you will still probably sense the changes and shifts in the harmony.

Also, in addition to expressing the harmony, this series of notes have a "musical train of thought"—a "flow" of ideas not simply played once and discarded, but utilizing motifs that are reused and developed over the course of the solo. This reuse and development of ideas is one hallmark of effective melodies, whether composed or improvised. To see just a few of the many manipulations of the similar ideas in the solo, look at figure 1.2.

Here are some of the types of variations used in the development of this solo:

a. transposed form

b. varied through interval changes

c. transposition to different chords and octaves

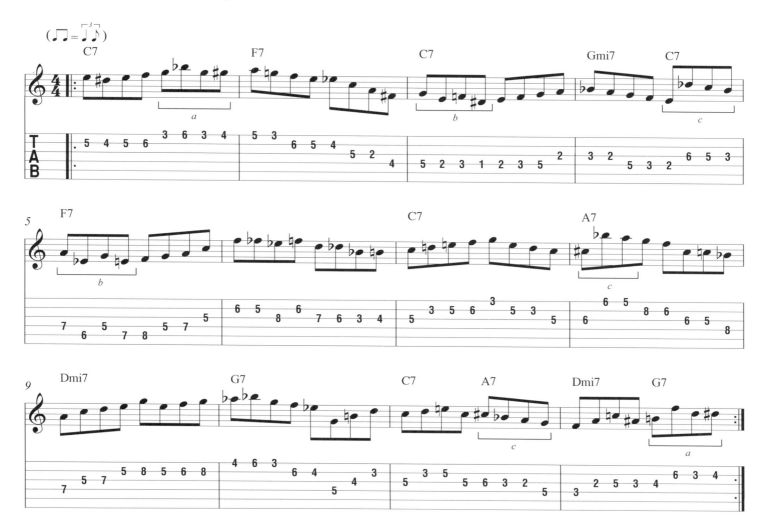

FIG. 1.2. Reuses of Ideas

Another important thing to notice is that the solo, despite a lack of rhythmic variety, has a noticeable *balance of pitch, range, and melodic shape*. While it contains some reuse of ideas, it is not overly repetitive. The flow of ideas in the solo takes the listener on a journey that is varied and interesting.

Look at the lines drawn over the notes in figure 1.3. If this were a hiking journey, it would have a nice balance of hills, valleys, and relatively level portions of the trip!

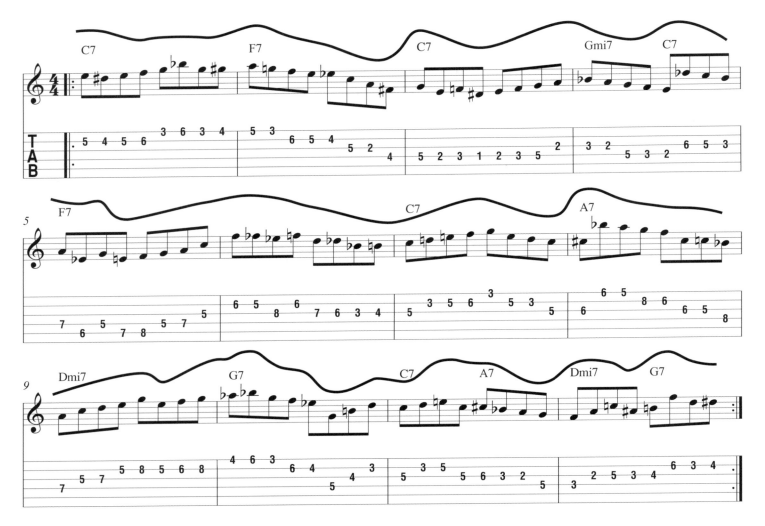

FIG. 1.3. Melodic Contour

Listening to and looking at these attributes, we can see the essential elements required to create a successful constant note value solo that "flows." These are:

- Harmonically related melody notes placed on downbeats and at points of chord change.

- Motivic idea(s) repeated and developed with variation techniques.

- Variety and balance of pitch range and melodic shape.

- And one final point: In 4/4 time, the building blocks of this technique can be identified as *four-note "cells,"* consisting of four contiguous eighth notes that can be repeated, reused, adapted, and reapplied. These are "portable" tools for building improvisational vocabulary.

These principles are not just used in jazz. They have been developed and refined for hundreds of years—for example, in the music of J. S. Bach, notably the *Six Partitas for Solo Violin*. I strongly encourage you to check out those masterful works and consider learning to play some of them on guitar! In doing so, you will not only learn examples of beautiful melodies that are harmonically descriptive; you will also likely improve your guitar technique as you navigate the technical challenges of the music. (Mark White's book *Jazz Guitar Fretboard Navigation: From Bach to Bebop*, Berklee Press 2016, explores these relationships in depth.)

Furthermore, and perhaps surprising to some, you will hear some sources of the jazz language in the music of Bach and other baroque composers. Many of the most influential jazz improvisers loved classical music and listened to it frequently. The list of jazz innovators influenced directly by classical music is long and includes Charlie Parker, John Coltrane, Duke Ellington, Keith Jarrett, and many others.

HOW DO WE EXPRESS HARMONY WITH MELODY?

By organizing the melody notes to support the harmonic changes in the given metrical structure, we can express the harmony while also building a melody. To discuss and understand this, let's define some terms and concepts.

Harmonically descriptive notes are notes that are either chord tones or tensions. The most descriptive are chord tones.

- *Chord tones* (CT) are the notes in the chord itself.

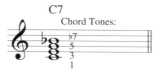

FIG. 1.4. Chord Tones of a Dominant Seventh Chord: 1, 3, 5, ♭7

- *Available tensions* (T) are extensions in thirds above the chord that support its harmonic function while adding color.

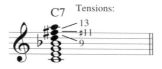

FIG. 1.5. One Possible Set of Tensions on a Dominant Seventh Chord: 9, #11, 13

Available tensions are *non-chord tones* that blend well when played along with the fundamental sound of the chord (i.e., the chord tones). The word "tension" is an abbreviation of the word "extension."

Seventh chords are built using intervals of a third from a root note. As you can see in figure 1.5, if we keep building on thirds beyond the 7, we get notes that are some form of 9, 11, and 13. A third above the 13 takes us back to the root (two octaves higher). Every chord, when extended like this, yields some form of 9, 11, 13.

Chord Scales

A *chord scale* is a concept for organizing melody/harmony relationships in an efficient visual way. If we arrange all of the stacked up (vertical) notes from our example chord C7(9,♯11,13) into a scale (horizontal) format, we get a "chord scale." This horizontal, scalar expression of the vertical stacked chord makes it easier to understand and "see" melodic/harmonic relationships. Available tensions are labeled with prefix "T" for tension. "Available" means that these tensions will blend well with the chord.

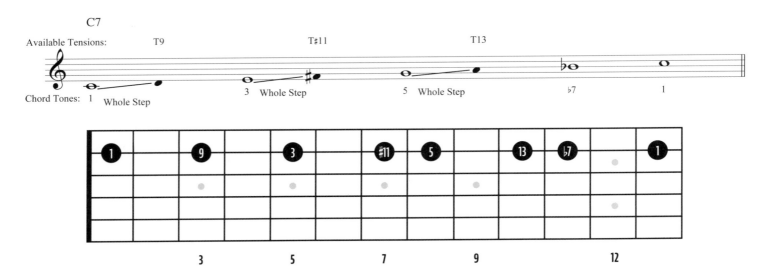

FIG. 1.6. One Possible Chord Scale for C7

Harmonic Avoid Notes

As the name implies, *harmonic avoid notes* (HAN) are non-chord tone notes that may be in a chord scale, but are dissonant against the chord in a way that weakens or destroys its harmonic function. They often sound like "wrong" notes, when emphasized against the chord of the moment. These are labeled with an "S" (meaning "scale" note), to be interpreted as "available in the scale, as a brief passing note, but not to be emphasized against the chord."

If we change the previous chord scale to another one that will also work with a C7 chord (e.g., the Mixolydian scale), we get an F instead of the previous F♯ as the fourth scale degree. That F is a harmonic avoid note and so is labeled "S4."

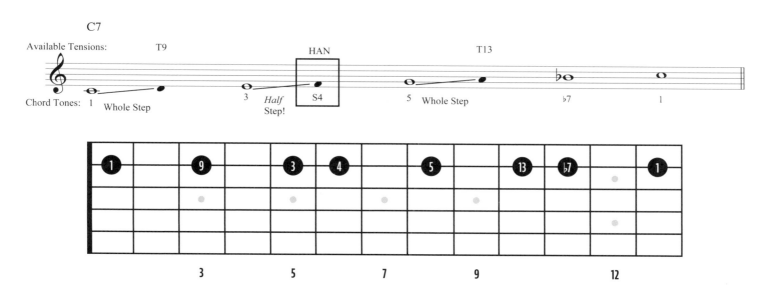

FIG. 1.7. Harmonic Avoid Note for C7/Mixolydian Chord Scale

Available Tensions vs. Harmonic Avoid Notes

For all chords (except certain dominant chords that will be dealt with later), the way we determine whether a given non-chord tone is an "available tension" (e.g., T9, T13, etc.) or a harmonic avoid note (e.g., S4) is this:

When the chord tones and potential tensions are viewed as a chord scale, available tensions are a *whole step* (two frets) above each chord tone.

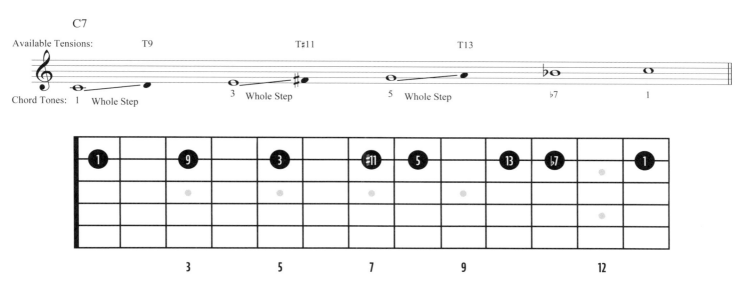

FIG. 1.8. C7 Available Tensions a Whole Step Above Each Chord Tone

Harmonic avoid notes are notes that are a *half step (one fret)* above a chord tone. An example of a diatonic harmonic avoid note is the F illustrated in figure 1.9.

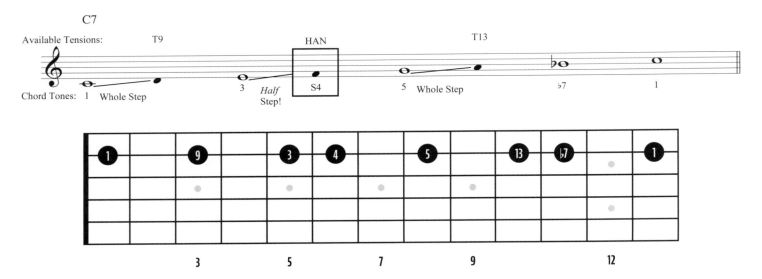

FIG. 1.9. Harmonic Avoid Note S4 on C7

Available tensions are labeled with numbers greater than 8 (T9, T11, T13, etc.). Harmonic avoid notes are labeled with numbers less than 8 (S4, S♭6, etc.).

Why does this rule work?

This approach is effective because half steps (minor seconds) and minor ninths (the expanded-by-an octave "compound" version of the half step) are significantly more dissonant than whole steps (or major ninths). Most chords are essentially consonant (relatively resolved sounding). The greater level of dissonance produced by a minor ninth is usually too much for most chords if they are to retain their essentially consonant harmonic function. Generally speaking, non-chord tone notes that are a half step above a chord tone (in chord scale format) are too dissonant to be emphasized effectively against most chords, most of the time. They are generally used as passing tones and placed on the upbeats (the "and" of beats).

Important Exception to the Rule: Dominant Chords

Dominant chords have a special dissonant and "restless" sound. Because the essential character of these chords *is* dissonant, certain types of extra dissonances can actually *reinforce* their function and help them sound even more restless, with more need for resolution. Therefore dominant chords *do* work well with certain tensions that are a half step (or minor ninth) above a chord tone, as in figure 1.10. In fact, these are *great* sounds!

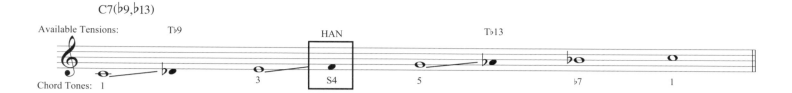

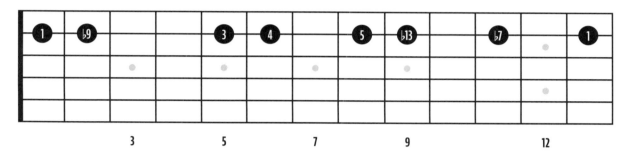

FIG. 1.10. C7(♭9,♭13) Chord Scale with S4

NOTE: In general, S4 is still not recommended as a featured dissonance on dominant seventh chords. Why? Because a main feature of dominant seventh chords is their ability to create expectation of resolution down a perfect fifth. That expectation is partly created by the 3 of the dominant chord, which acts as the "leading tone" (a note leading the ear upward by a half step to the root of the target chord). *S4 is that target note*—the note which the leading tone is leading to, the root of the target chord down a P5.

Mixing S4 with the 3, in the harmony, or in a featured melody note against the harmony, can dilute and weaken the drama of that leading function, sort of like mixing the "answer" in with the question, or a punch line in with the setup of a joke. You lose the suspense of expectation because you are already hearing the goal note featured too soon.

So, use S4 as a passing tone, not a goal note. This is just a general guideline though. At faster tempos, the effect of S4 is a bit less obvious, and sometimes players will intentionally target this dissonance and quickly resolve it for effect—common in traditional blues, for example.

ANALYSIS TERMINOLOGY

chord tones: (CT)	Notes of the basic chord up to the 7 (or 6 if it has a 6 instead of a 7).
available tensions: (T)	Non-chord tones, from the chord scale, which work well with the basic sound of the chord and add "color" to the overall sound. These are numbered as various forms of 9, 11, and 13 (T9, T11, T13).
harmonic avoid notes: (S or HAN)	Non-chord tones, from the chord scale, which do not work well with the basic chord sound. These are numbered with scale degree/interval numbers less than 8, e.g., "S4" or "S♭6" etc.
chord scale:	A series of notes, represented horizontally in scale form, which effectively convey the sound and function of a chord along with scale passing tones (HANs) and available tensions (T).

EXPRESSING HARMONY WITH MELODY

Here are some basic guidelines for expressing harmony with the melody—the key to creating "flow."

In 4/4 time, when using primarily sub-metrical melody note values (eighth notes in 4/4 time), beats 1 and 3 are strongest and are the primary downbeats. Beats 2 and 4 are still relatively strong because they are also downbeats on pulses in the meter but are a bit weaker than 1 and 3, so 2 and 4 are secondary downbeats in 4/4. All downbeats are "anchor" points. The "ands" (upbeats or halfway points between each downbeat) are weak points and are "transitional" in function. They are unanchored points in the meter. NOTE: *It is possible to make upbeats into target points via anticipation and syncopation. This will be discussed later in the book.*

1. Harmonically descriptive notes (chord tones and available tensions) should occur on the strong points—the pulses in a given metrical structure (i.e., the "downbeats").

In figure 1.11, the notes on the metrically "strong" points are all harmonically "descriptive" (they convey important elements of the overall chord sound). We'll call these notes placed on strong points "target notes."

Audio 5

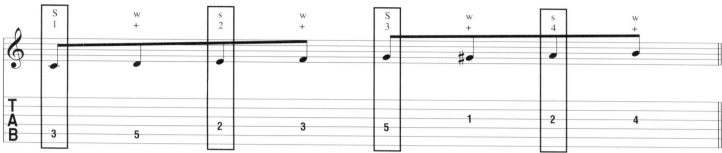

FIG. 1.11. Chord Tones and Tensions on Strong Locations in the Beat

2. Harmonic avoid notes and notes outside the chord scale should be placed on "weak" metrical points—i.e., the "and" of each beat in 4/4 time. Chord tones and tensions can also be placed on weak points but the less descriptive notes definitely should be placed on the "ands." Again the downbeats are strong, goal sounds to the ear; all the "ands" (upbeats) are weak or "transitional" in sound.

Notes—whether chord tones, tensions, or passing tones—that occur on "weak" metric points and which resolve by step into the next note are termed "approach notes."

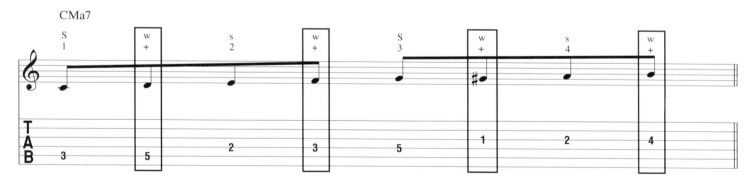

FIG. 1.12. Approach Notes on Weak Metric Points

Notice that the G♯, which could be thought of as a "wrong" note against the CMa7 chord (since it's neither a chord tone nor an available tension), sounds fine because of its metrical placement. It's on a weak point—an "and" upbeat—so the ear perceives this note as a link, not a destination. The "wrong note" G♯ does not sound wrong here *because of its metrical placement*. It is functioning as an *approach* note.

Here are the first four bars of "Blues in C" showing how the notes can be analyzed. We will discuss all of these concepts later in the book.

FIG. 1.13. "Blues in C" Measures 1 to 4 Annotated

TO SUM UP: BOTH *WHAT* AND *WHERE* MATTER

What notes you play is important—but also, *where* (in the meter) you play a given note is important.

As you progress through this book you'll learn to use this information to create solos that are both effective as melodies and, simultaneously, reflective of the underlying harmony.

IMPROVISING USING CONSTANT NOTE VALUES

Why restrict yourself to constant eighth notes when all your favorite solos feature rhythmic variety? The answer may seem paradoxical:

Well-chosen limits help us learn and be creative. Temporary limitation leads ultimately to greater freedom.

Limitation is a learning technique—an empowering *means to an end*, and often, a part of the creative development process.

The limitation of having to improvise in constant eighth notes (or any constant note value) requires that we deal effectively with melody/harmony relationships. Consequently, when rhythmic variation is added back into the mix, the player has greater control and freedom.

Four-Notes Cells as Building Blocks

In our first example solo (figure 1.1), we outlined some related note groupings. Some consisted of four notes and some of eight, but all of them—indeed, every measure of the solo—can be understood in terms of four-note cells (the eight-note portions are simply two four-note cells grouped together).

To continue our analogy relating musical improvisation to spoken language, these four-note cells are like "words," which can be then formed into phrases and sentences.

There are a number of resources a player needs to use to construct the various four-note cells. These include primarily:

- scales

- arpeggios

- approach tones and approach-tone patterns

- chromatic linking devices and gestures

A large proportion of "jazz" or melodic improvisational vocabulary is derived from various combinations of these sources.

Learning every scale, arpeggio, approach tone pattern, and chromatic device in the abstract before applying them to music would be like trying to learn a language by reading a dictionary; you would be overwhelmed long before you could express yourself meaningfully in the language!

The approach of this book is to get you "speaking" small segments of the language quickly, giving you a limited, but flexible and useful vocabulary. After experiencing some success within these limits, you will gain momentum toward the task of building broader and deeper vocabulary.

A component of this strategy is to package initial vocabulary into four-note cells.

For example, in the previous solo (figure 1.1), these resources were used and reused multiple times in the form of easily understandable and portable four-note cells. Just a sampling are indicated.

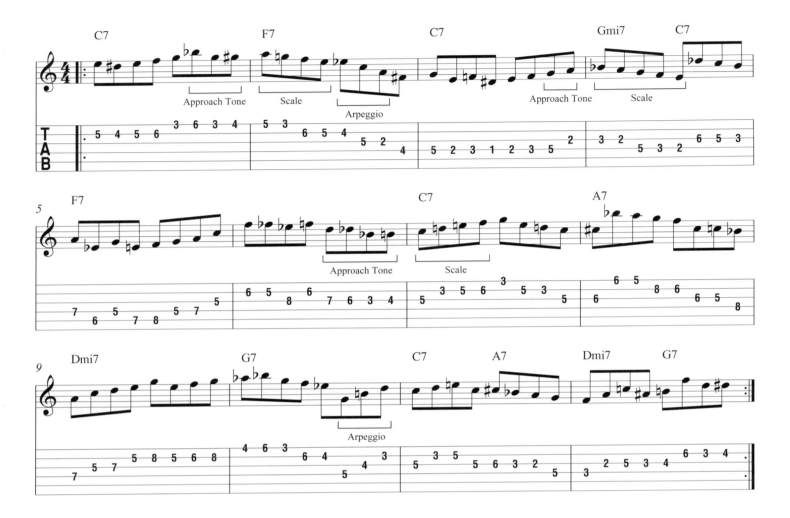

FIG. 1.14. Four-Note Cells in "Blues in C"

When used with the guidelines we're about to learn, each of these are building blocks that can be "plugged in" to a solo and used—almost like a chord voicing or chord shape on the guitar—to get from one idea to the next smoothly. They work well for two reasons:

- Note content supports the harmonic function of the chord of the moment.
- Organization of notes in the metric structure is effective at expressing the harmony. Important and harmonically descriptive notes on downbeats and transitional notes on upbeats.

Each of these cell types will be explored in more detail, in later chapters. First, we will look at practical ways to learn two of the most basic of these resources: scales and arpeggios. What follows is one way to efficiently and practically organize our learning of these resources, specifically on the guitar.

CHAPTER 2

Organizing Scales and Arpeggios

ERGONOMIC FINGERINGS ON GUITAR

There are many ways to approach the learning of scales on the guitar because the guitar is a complex instrument. It operates in more than one "dimension" in terms of pitch. Its standard tuning has a problematic asymmetry, and there are multiple ways to play most of its pitches.

Guitarists need to have strategies to deal with these challenges in order to become effective improvisers.

Unlike the piano keyboard, where movement to the right produces upward pitch only and leftward movement produces downward pitch, the guitar has two ways to go up in pitch and two ways to go down.

Vertical movement facilitates going up or down in pitch.

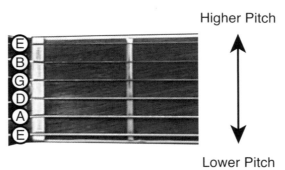

FIG. 2.1. Vertical Movement

But so does *horizontal* movement.

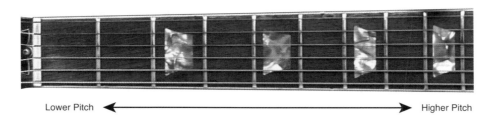

FIG. 2.2. Horizontal Movement

The *tuning* of the guitar is not consistent. Most strings are tuned a perfect fourth apart, except for the major third between the third (G) and second (B) strings.

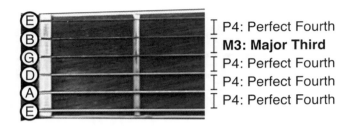

FIG. 2.3. Standard Tuning

Additionally, there are multiple places where we can access the same note on the fretboard.

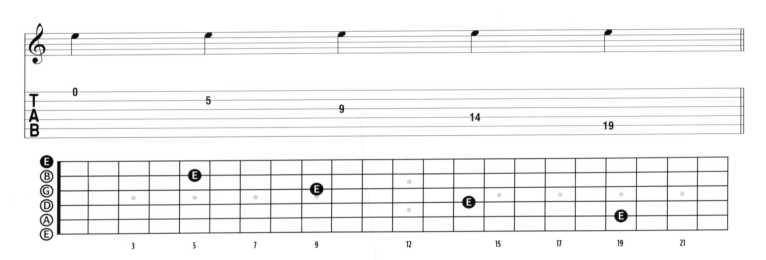

FIG. 2.4. High E at Five String Locations

SOLUTION: THINK IN TERMS OF STRING SETS

One way to deal with this challenge is to break down the fretboard into "string sets," or subgroups of adjacent strings. By so doing, we can learn a scale, lick, arpeggio, etc. in a smaller "chunk" and then move it to other string sets until we eventually link the whole fretboard.

NOTE: What follows are strategies for mapping the fretboard to help in the process of learning to improvise over changes. There are many other approaches and fingerings that are of additional value. Once you can find your way around the fretboard, I encourage you to investigate some of the other helpful approaches.

Scales

Use this one-octave major-scale shape and move it to all string sets, adjusting for the tuning anomaly between strings 3 and 2.

Here is the shape, with the scale degrees labeled.

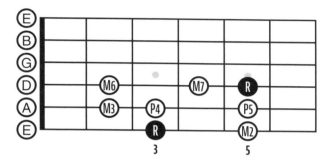

FIG. 2.5. Major Scale Shape with Scale Degrees

Here is the shape on strings ⑥⑤④ (G major) and ⑤④③ (C major). Notice that these string sets share the same fingering pattern for a major scale.

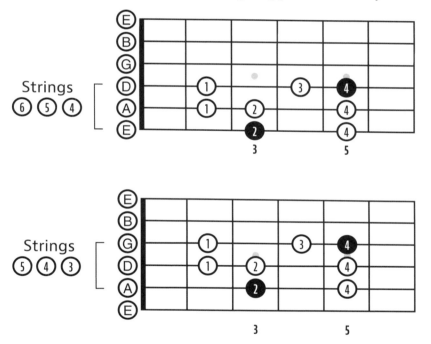

FIG. 2.6. String Sets ⑥⑤④ and ⑤④③ Share Common Fingering Patterns

On string set ④③② (F major), note the change of the fingering pattern to accommodate the strings 3–2 tuning anomaly. The formula for this is: when moving toward the high E string, as you encounter the second string, move previous fingering up one fret to make up for the "lost" half step. (A major third is a half step less than a perfect fourth.)

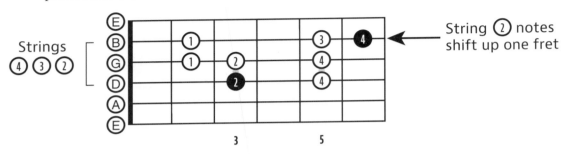

FIG. 2.7. String Set ④③②

String set ③②① (A major) is another note fingering variation. Notice the adjustment on the second string fingering pattern.

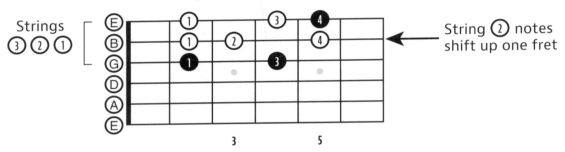

FIG. 2.8. String Set ③②①

PICKING AND ARTICULATION OF ONE-OCTAVE SCALE FORMS

Expressive and musical playing uses a mixture of articulation techniques, such as alternate picking, economy picking, and legato. Picked notes create accents and percussive sounds. For guitar players who want to imitate the phrasing of horn players, integration of at least some legato elements is important.

Linking One-Octave Cells While Practicing Horizontal Shifts

There are many ways to organize scales on the guitar, but I've chosen to highlight the one-octave cell idea because it relates to strategy 2, "Break It Down." It's a strategy for *learning and connecting* the entire neck with a small amount of material.

Guitarists often get trapped in a few comfortable positions and neglect material that *links* different areas of the neck. These one-octave cells can be practiced in a way that helps the player get comfortable with more horizontal movement via shifts.

Below is one possible fingering solution that can be applied.

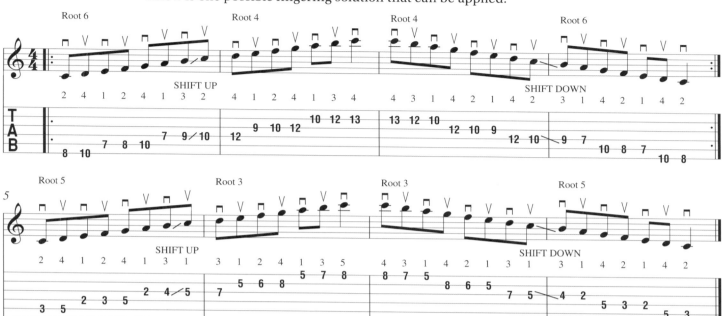

FIG. 2.9. Root 6 Linked to Root 4, and Root 5 Linked to Root 3

There are many ways to finger scales on the guitar, and eventually, all of them should be explored to allow complete freedom on the instrument. The one-octave scale approach is here for its mapping value. It makes small, portable scale "chunks" easier to learn and to transpose. All other ideas, whether scale- or arpeggio-based, can be related to them and thus be easier to remember and contextualize. Regardless of whether you choose to practice these scale cells for technique benefits, they are worth learning for their scale visualization and transposition value.

ARPEGGIO ORGANIZATION ON GUITAR: "ERGONOMIC" ARPEGGIOS 4x4x4

The "4x4x4" system is a way to learn to play arpeggios of multiple chord structures from *any* finger on *any* string on *any* part of the neck and link any combination of arpeggios over the entire neck.

There are:

- four possible starting fingers on the fretting hand (1, 2, 3, 4)
- four notes in a seventh chord arpeggio (e.g., CMa7 = C, E, G, B)
- four string sets of three adjacent strings (⑥⑤④, ⑤④③, ④③②, ③②①)

We'll begin with the four most commonly used seventh chords:

- Major 7 = 1 3 5 7
- Dominant 7 = 1 3 5 ♭7
- Minor 7 = 1 ♭3 5 ♭7
- Minor 7♭5 = 1 ♭3 ♭5 ♭7

Once you are comfortable with these, it's easy to apply the learning process to any others. The following exercises are four-note cells, playing the same arpeggios using different fingerings. In some cases, the chord is transposed up an octave to avoid open-string voicings.

String Set ⑥⑤④ (Root ⑥)

FIG. 2.10. C Arpeggio on Strings ⑥⑤④

String Set ③②① (Root ③)

FIG. 2.13. C Arpeggio on String Set ③②①

Next, practice from each finger to a cycle-V backing track. Here are the major 7 chords starting from the first finger, to get you started. Practice it on all chord types, from all roots, starting from every finger.

FIG. 2.14. Cycle-V Exercise on Major 7 Chords

Next try playing the arpeggios within a limited area of the neck. Choose each new starting figure in such a way as to minimize horizontal motion. This will force you to find solutions within a limited area of the neck and thus learn each area thoroughly. Practice this along with tracks 6 and 7.

FIG. 2.15. Ergonomic Arpeggios

APPLYING BASIC ARPEGGIO SHAPES TO CHORD PROGRESSIONS AS PREPARATION FOR IMPROVISATION

Below are a few practice approaches that apply the arpeggio shapes to chord progressions. Practicing these kinds of routines is valuable in a variety of ways. In doing so, you:

1. Map out the most fundamental notes of the harmony (which you'll need to access when you improvise).

2. Reinforce your ability to "hear" (internally "audiate") the harmonic structure as you practice. Being able to pre-hear the changes in your head allows you to do more than just avoid wrong notes; it is what is required to create melodic ideas that flow organically with a musical train of thought.

When you are familiar with the shapes, begin applying them to standard, common progressions like the ones listed later in this book (chapter 7). Here is an example over "Rhythm Changes."

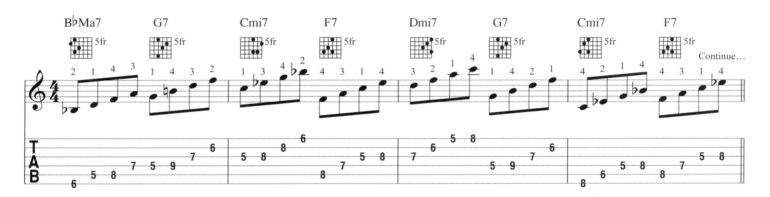

FIG. 2.16. Arpeggios over "Rhythm Changes"

Audio 8

Next, try arranging the notes of each arpeggio so that you can move by step from the end of one arpeggio to the start of the next—again, by step, as much as possible. At this point, the exercise will begin to sound a bit more like real jazz improvised vocabulary.

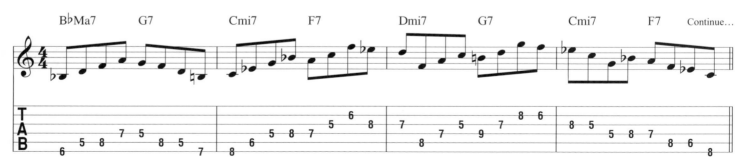

FIG. 2.17. Approaching New Arpeggios by Step

Audio 9

For an even more musical effect, experiment with octave displacement and note order of selected notes in the arpeggios, to achieve more variation in melodic shape.

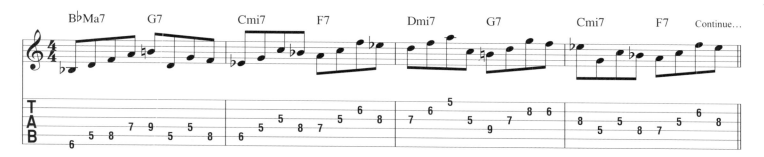

FIG. 2.18. Displaced Octaves

LINKING ARPEGGIO SHAPES ACROSS STRING SETS

Work toward being able to access all the shapes on the neck. Practice "seeing" shapes across octaves and string sets.

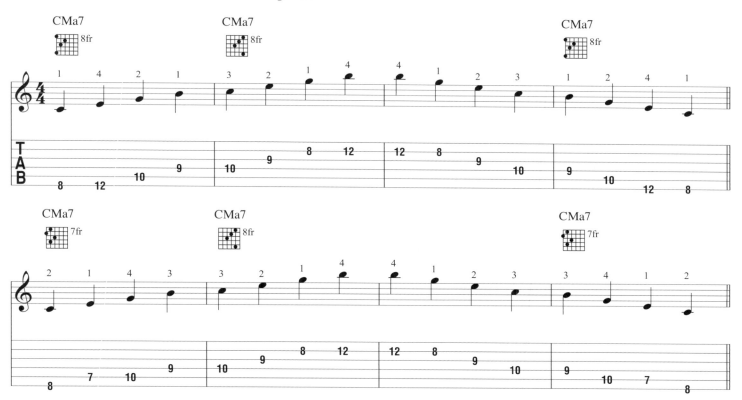

FIG. 2.19. Linking Arpeggio Shapes Across String Sets. In this case, we are linking the shape for root 6 to the shape for root 4.

SUPERIMPOSING ARPEGGIOS TO ACCESS MORE TENSIONS

Next, we again apply basic arpeggio shapes to chord progressions, but now, as chord superimpositions to help us access more "color" notes—i.e., tensions.

A wonderful bonus to learning arpeggios is that they are multi-use. They give a lot of return on the investment of time spent learning them because they can be used for purposes beyond accessing the basic chord sound.

As discussed, arpeggios are a series of stacked thirds. If you keep building thirds, you create upper extensions (tensions), also built on thirds. These upper structures are just other seventh chords. If you play an Emi7 against a CMa7 chord, the sound produced will be the notes E, G, B, D against CMa7, producing CMa7(9).

In this way, we can superimpose arpeggios starting on any note (not just the root) of a chord. In so doing we access *upper extensions* of the chord.

If we are playing over a CMa7 chord, we can use arpeggios we've already learned to access tensions on the chord in the following way.

Basic Seventh Chord	Related Seventh Chord Based on the 3	Related Seventh Chord Based on the 5	Related Seventh Chord Based on the 7
Ma7	mi7	dominant 7	mi7♭5
CMa7	Emi7	G7	Bmi7♭5
C E G B 1 3 5 7	E G B D 3 5 7 9	G B D F 5 7 9 11	B D F A 7 9 11 13

In this way, we can multiply the uses for each arpeggio and access some hip sounds (9, 11, 13) quite easily. NOTE: Some upper-extension notes from a given superimposed arpeggio may turn out to be harmonic avoid notes. This is the case here with the note F on CMa7 (it is S4). Therefore, we need to learn to use only the upper-structure arpeggios that contain exclusively "available" notes on a given chord. In the above chart, only Emi7 is practical to superimpose on CMa7. This is a big topic, but for now, let's focus on just one of these options: the arpeggio based on the 3 of the basic chord.

Choose an arpeggio, based on the original chord's 3, which is *from the chord scale that you want to color the chord with*. Usually, this would be a diatonic chord in the same key for example, in the key of C you could superimpose Emi7 against CMa7. Both chords are diatonic to C. The resulting composite sound would be C, E, G, B, D, i.e., CMa7(9). Usually the chord chosen is the diatonic chord built on another chord tone (3, 5, 7), but particularly on dominant chords, it often sounds great to choose non-diatonic chords that yield altered tensions. Here, we'll focus on superimpositions built on the chord's 3.

To get started let's use these arpeggios on a few of the chords from B♭ "Rhythm Changes." The superimposed arpeggios all yield three chord tones plus a tension 9.

Basic Seventh Chord	Seventh Chord from the 3 of Basic Chord	Notes Yielded
B♭Ma7	use Dmi7	D F A C 3 5 7 9
G7	use Bmi7♭5	B D F A 3 5 ♭7 9
Cmi7	use E♭Ma7	E♭ G B♭ D ♭3 5 ♭7 9
F7	use Ami7♭5	A C E♭ G 3 5 ♭7 9

Superimposing Arpeggios from the 3 of the Basic Chord

Audio 10

Try this exercise first.

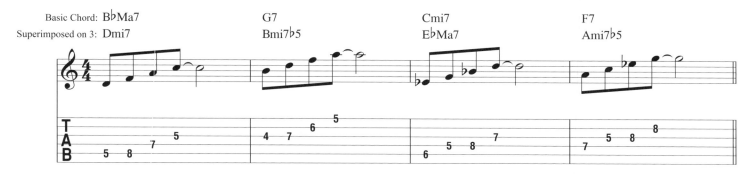

FIG. 2.20. Superimposed Arpeggios

Audio 11

Then chain some of these superimposed arpeggios.

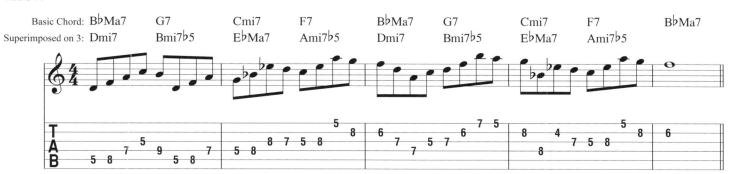

FIG. 2.21. Chained Arpeggios

The sound of these superimposed seventh chords, derived from the 3 of the underlying chord, produce more color than basic 1, 3, 5, 7 arpeggios because they include the 9 instead of the root.

There are many creative ways to use arpeggios to create interesting improvised melodies. A whole world of useful improvisational language can be derived from arpeggios. We'll be investigating some more applications later in this book. The serious student is encouraged to continue to include arpeggio practice in every study session and to continue to explore their creative use.

CHAPTER 3

Common Chord Patterns and Progressions

Eventually, we would like to be able to improvise over any chord progression, but it makes most practical sense to build a foundation by initially working with some of the most commonly used chord patterns, progressions that are the foundation of hundreds of variations.

CIRCLE OF FIFTHS

The *circle of fifths* is a way to organize your thinking about music and is an essential tool that all musicians can use to their benefit. It is related to the overtone series and many chord progressions are organized around it, when they utilize consecutive chords with roots proceeding down in perfect fifths. This is called "cycle V" root motion.

There are countless ways to use and practice this cycle, and I encourage you to learn it, be able to draw it from memory, and continue to investigate the many ways in which it reflects and informs our understanding of music.

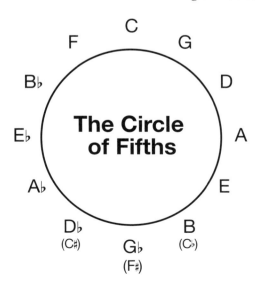

FIG. 3.1. Circle of Fifths

In this book, we'll refer to this cycle as a way to think about movement between chord roots and keys.

Chord movement *down* a perfect fifth (counterclockwise, on figure 3.1) is extremely common. This is true particularly of dominant seventh chords, but it is also common with other chord types too. For this reason, many of the exercises in this book will be applied to the circle of fifths (or "cycle V") in some way.

Below is one example of applying arpeggio derived four-note cells to the cycle. Remember that in order to attain "flow" and freedom improvising on guitar, we need to be able to play any idea with multiple fingerings and in a variety of locations on the neck. Later in this book, I will show fingering strategies that allow that comprehensive approach. For now, by way of an introduction to the concept and sound, this example shows only a few fingering options and is limited to about a five-fret area.

Audio 12

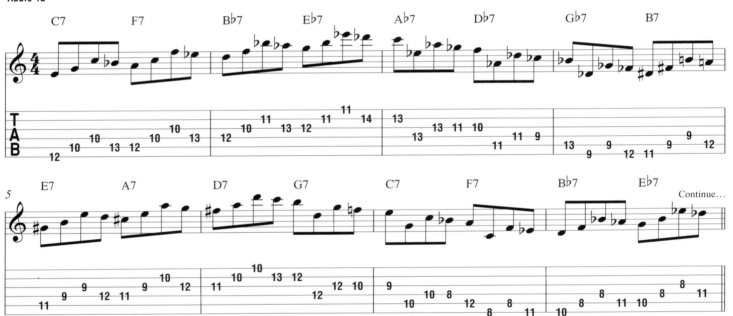

FIG. 3.2. Four-Note Cells on a Cycle-V Progression

MAJOR AND MINOR TWO-FIVES

The "two-five" (II V) progression is a term referring to the diatonic chords built on scale degree 2 (the II chord) and scale degree 5 (the V chord) of a major or minor scale. The II and V chords are often played in succession thus creating a "two-five." Two-fives are extremely common in jazz as well as many other genres. These two particular chords played in succession form a powerful harmonic unit, and when the dominant 7 chord resolves down a perfect fifth, it's even more powerful.

Major Two-Five Progression

Harmonic functions are terms used to describe the relative consonance and dissonance of chords in a key. The IImi7 to V7 to IMa7 incorporates *all the three harmonic functions*, taking the listener on a kind of journey, to "away from home" (subdominant), to "very unstable, wanting to go home" (dominant), to "home, resolved sounding" (tonic).

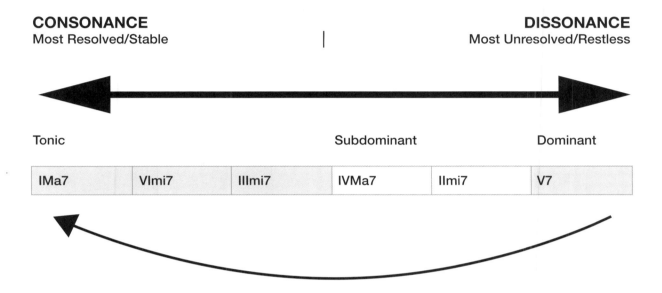

FIG. 3.3. Chord Function and Dissonance

If we look at this in the key of C major, the chords would be:

FIG. 3.4. IImi7 V7 IMa7 in C Major

If we relate this to the circle of fifths, we can see that the root motion of this progression is "riding" the circle counterclockwise (down a perfect fifth).

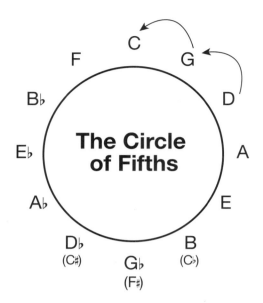

FIG. 3.5. Root Motion of II V I Down Circle of Fifths

The two-five progression (II V I, in its full form) is common because it:

- Incorporates all three harmonic functions and thus has a balance of tension and resolution built in to it.

- Makes use of the inherent momentum of cycle-V root motion.

APPLYING FOUR-NOTE CELLS TO MAJOR II V I PROGRESSION

Here's one of many possibilities to apply four-note cells to a IImi7 V7 progression. Let's use one arpeggio cell and one scale cell to create an effective set of notes to reflect the underlying harmony.

Audio 13

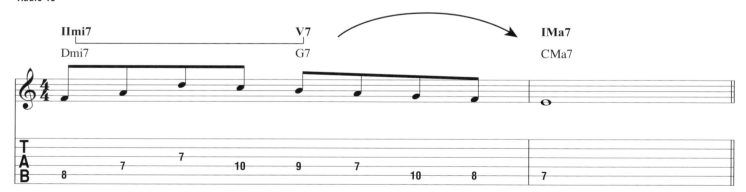

FIG. 3.6. Four-Note Cells in a IImi7 V7 IMa7 Progression

Minor Two-Five Progression

Whenever a mi7 or mi7♭5 chord precedes a dominant 7 chord in a counterclockwise cycle-V root pattern, the two chords form a two-five relationship. Look for two-fives in all the following chord patterns.

First, here's the two-five lick from figure 3.6 applied to a minor version of the II V I progression.

Audio 14

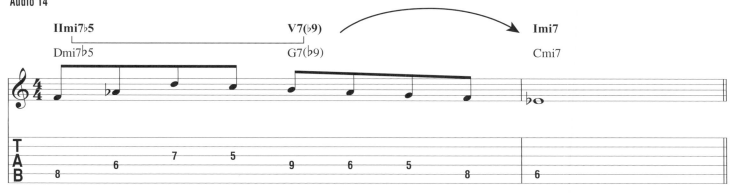

FIG. 3.7. Four-Note Cells in a IImi7♭5 V7(♭9) Imi7 Progression

"RHYTHM CHANGES"

"Rhythm Changes" is the aforementioned chord progression framework based on Gershwin's "I Got Rhythm." There are many variations; we'll stick to a common version, shown in figure 3.8. It's a 32-bar A1 A2 B1 A2 form. Here, it's in the key of B♭ major (most common key). Once you know it well in B♭, you should transpose it to all keys.

Audio 15

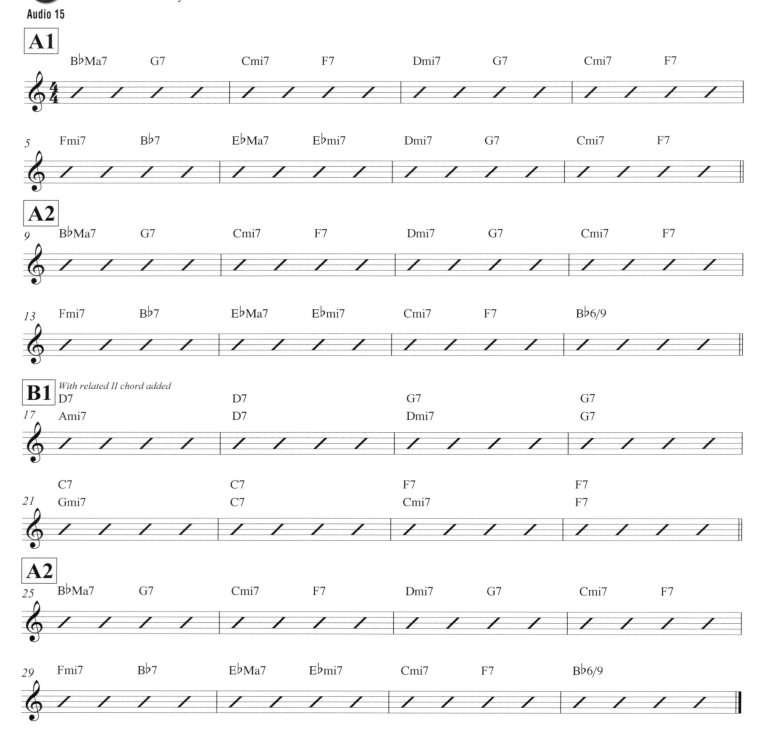

FIG. 3.8. "Rhythm Changes"

"JAZZ BLUES"

Audio 16

The most basic blues progression uses only three dominant seventh chords: I7, IV7, and V7. In jazz blues, related IImi7 chords and secondary dominants are added, and chord changes become more frequent. As with "Rhythm Changes," there are many variations possible, but the most common set of changes for jazz players is below in figure 3.9. We'll refer to it as "Jazz Blues" changes in this book. In a typical jazz jam session, if a blues is called, chances are it will use these changes or a close variant.

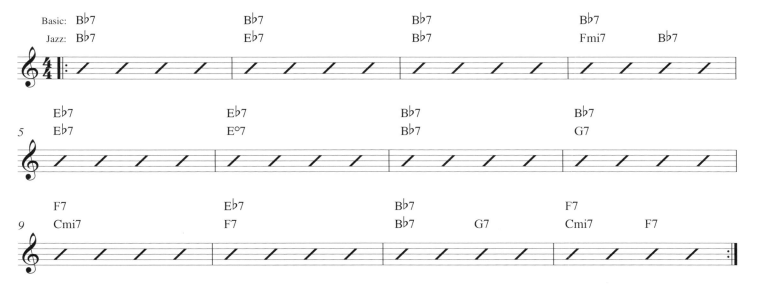

FIG. 3.9. "Jazz Blues" Progression

"BIRD BLUES"

The name "Bird Blues" comes from the great jazz innovator who first used this elaborate reharmonization of the blues: virtuoso saxophonist Charles "Yardbird" Parker, a founding member of the bebop movement in jazz. Parker used this set of changes to underpin many of his most famous blues compositions, including perhaps his most famous blues: "Blues for Alice."

Play through chords of the "Bird Blues" listed below. It's a different sound. More chord types have been added (Ma7, mi7♭5), there are many two-fives now, and the overall harmonic rhythm has increased to two chords per measure. You may wonder how this much more complex set of changes can even be labeled a "blues." In spite of these new elements, many of the basic aural sign posts of the blues are still present. Those are:

- a twelve-bar form
- a I chord at measure 1
- a IV chord at measure 5
- a cadence involving the V chord beginning at measure 9

Audio 17

"Bird Blues" changes are ideal for learning to improvise over fast-moving changes.

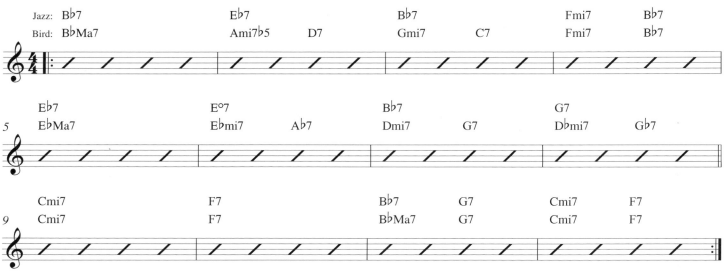

FIG. 3.10. "Bird Blues" Compared to "Jazz Blues"

COLTRANE'S MULTITONIC CHORD CHANGES

Jazz giant saxophonist/composer John Coltrane spent much of his musical life exploring symmetry in musical forms, specifically symmetrical scales, and the harmony derived from them. In various compositions, including his landmark "Giant Steps," Coltrane explored the even division of the octave. In "Giant Steps," the focus is major third intervals. (The key centers in figure 3.11 are B, G, Eb, which divide the octave evenly into major third segments.) This kind of composition uses a *multitonic* system: an organization of harmony that allows for multiple notes in symmetrical relationship to become the tonic, or root note of a key. The key centers trade off with each other creating in aggregate the effect of more than one tonic, a series of equal but different tonics, i.e., "multitonic." Again, here, the tonal centers are B major, G major and Eb major, the notes of the symmetrical augmented triad. The harmonies introduced in this system of "Coltrane Changes" became very influential and are now commonly used for composition and to reharmonize standard tunes.

Don't be intimidated! Yes, playing over these changes is more challenging than the others listed, but the tools you will get from this book—and from studying Coltrane's own solos—will allow you to develop fluency improvising over them with practice. Once you get used to the highly pattern-based harmonic shifts, it becomes easier. . . and there are a lot of two-fives integrated into it!

Audio 18

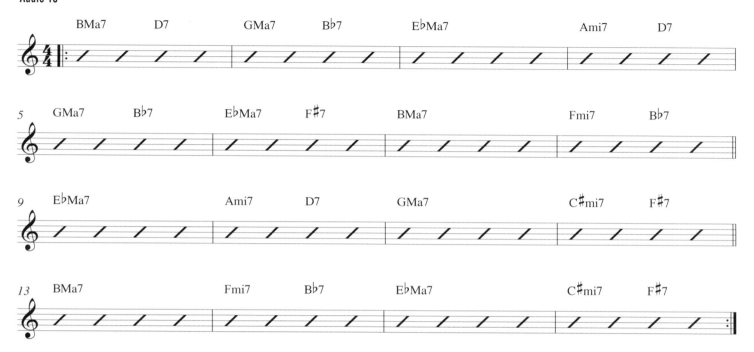

FIG. 3.11. "Coltrane" Changes

CHAPTER 4

Guidelines for Developing Melodic/ Harmonic "Flow"

EFFECTIVE CONSTANT NOTE-VALUE SOLO ATTRIBUTES

In chapter 1, we looked at the "Blues in C" solo, which is comprised of only eighth notes. In that chapter, I related, in a general way, some of the attributes of the solo that help make it an effective combination of melodic and harmonic material. Now, we're ready to specifically define the attributes that make a constant note-value solo effective. Again, constant note-value improvising is a means to an end to help improvisers attain skill and fluency. Great solos will always ultimately have rhythmic variety. And remember, "constant note value" can apply to both straight and swing (♫ = ♩♪) performances of eighth-note or sixteenth-note values.

Here are some of the attributes of effective constant note-value solos:

- **Voice Leading.** Stepwise motion at point of chord change (most of the time).

- **Harmony/Melodic Rhythm Relationship.** Chord tones/available tensions occur on downbeats. Placing harmonically descriptive notes on these important rhythmic markers is essential to having your lines connect to and "describe" the changes.

- **Leaps.** Leaps go from CT or T to a CT or T. When leaping, the note choices at either end of the leap tend to *sound emphasized* to the listener. Start by learning to use chord tones or available tensions at these points.

NOTE: When exceptions to this occur, it's usually to a suspension or dissonance that is then immediately resolved, usually in the opposite direction from the leap. More on this later.

- **Tension/Resolution.** More tension tends to be used at ends of phrases, right before resolutions to new chords—especially those using dominant chords. This added tension is often created with chromatic and/or "altered" tones. This is like a story that builds up tension right before the satisfying conclusion. If the chromatics create a "darker" sound and the resolution is "brighter," then one way to relate to this is the phrase "It's darkest before the dawn."

- **Motivic thinking.** Since in constant-note soloing there are no rhythm motives, it's particularly important that pitch motives are being used and reused via development techniques such as sequence, inversion, etc.

- **Balance of horizontal with vertical.** Over the course of a solo and often even over just one chorus, there is a balance of arpeggio-based (horizontal) and linear-based (scalar/chromatic) ideas.

Regarding the attributes discussed earlier in this chapter:

1. **Voice leading** is used at every chord change, thus "guiding" the ear to the next sound and creating a smooth transition between chord changes.

2. **Chord tones** (and some available tensions) are on downbeats (beats 1, 2, 3, 4), which are experienced by the listener as more "defining" of the harmony. Only one harmonic avoid note is on a downbeat (the F on the C7 chord beat 2, measure 3), but it is justified and sounds effective because it is part of an approach tone pattern (an "enclosure" or "surround"), which makes sense of, and resolves, the dissonance.

3. **Leaps** are between available notes (chord tones and tensions). Leaps emphasize notes to the ear, so generally, you don't want to leap out of, or into, harmonic avoid notes (unless you are going for a dissonant special effect).

4. **Consonance/dissonance.** Not a rule, just an effective practice, it's common to use more altered or dissonant tensions toward the end of a phrase because, when the melodic line does subsequently resolve, the contrast of dissonance to consonance heightens the impact of the resolution.

5. **Reuse/development of melodic material.** There are multiple reuses and variations on melodic material even within this four-measure excerpt. Among these are the labeled sequences (melodic fragments, with same interval structure, transposed to different starting points).

Audio 19

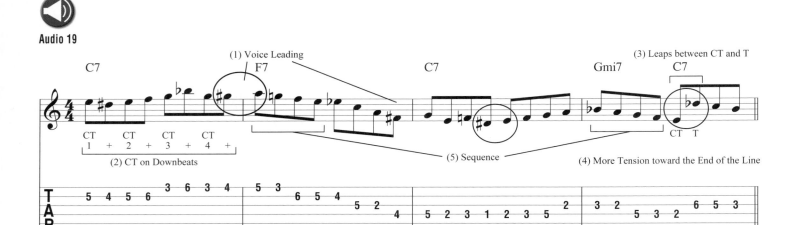

FIG. 4.1. Annotated Melody

An effective way to organize our melodic material is in terms of four-note cells. Using the previously described chord scale labeling language, we can analyze notes against the "chord of the moment." In figure 4.2, take a look at some of the most commonly used four-note cells.

COMMON TYPES OF FOUR-NOTE CELLS

Four-Note Cells	Description	Example	Notated
Arpeggios (basic)	1, 3, 5, 7 of the chord of the moment.	C7 = C, E, G, B♭	
Arpeggios (upper structures)	Using arpeggios of other chords superimposed to add tensions including 9, 11, 13, or alterations.	D7 superimposed on C7 which creates 9, #11, 13	
Scale (stepwise)	A series of stepwise notes moving through the chord scale of the moment	C7 scale four-note cells = C, D, E, F (up); C, B♭, A, G (down); or any of the possibilities moving up or down stepwise	
Scale (pattern based)	A series of notes using a discernable interval pattern, such as thirds, fourths, etc.	C7 scale ascending or descending in thirds, fourths, or other consistent intervals	
Bebop Scales	Common diatonic scales + 1 chromatic note. Taken as a whole this is not a four-note cell but the scale can be divided into two four-note "tetrachords" to incorporate it into the system of tools.	Most common are Mixolydian: 1 2 3 4 5 6 ♭7 **7** 1 Ionian: 1 2 3 4 5 **#5** 6 7 1 Dorian: 1 2 ♭3 4 5 6 ♭7 **7** 1	
Approach-Tone Patterns	Heavily used in bebop and other styles. If the four-note cell is a combo of chord tones and chromatic linking notes, it's often using an "approach-tone pattern."		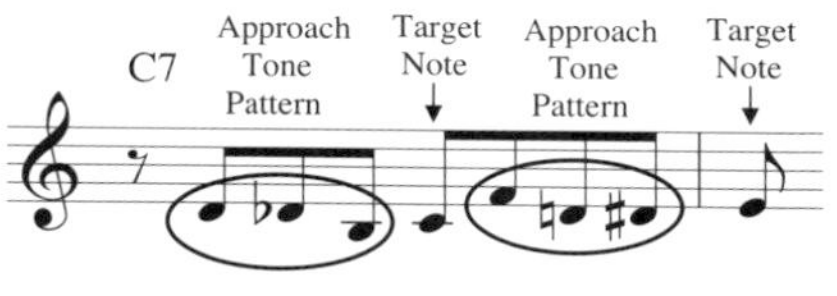
"Number" (aka "Digital") Patterns	Scale fragments, which may or may not move stepwise.	1 2 3 5 on a given chord	
Chromatic "Connector" Cells	Often used to "float" chromatically over the changes with an eventual resolution (usually via half step) to a solid "anchor" tone (CT or T).		

FIG. 4.2. Types of Four-Note Cells

CHAPTER 5

From a Grain of Sand

I want to share a great melodic phrase that has been around for hundreds of years. I call it the "primordial lick" to help convey its connection to the history of western music. It's a collection of notes that are a great model for a melodic line that flows descriptively and melodically through a set of chord changes. It works so well that I'm recommending that you learn this one lick over the whole guitar neck! Utilizing this small fragment, you can unlock the fretboard and open many pathways to improvising over changing harmony on the guitar. From a grain of sand, the universe.

To accomplish this will require a flexible approach to fingering. Developing an understanding of how to be flexible with fingerings on guitar will help you to ultimately achieve greater creative freedom. Before launching into the musical examples, we need to look at strategies that help you achieve fluidity and flexibility with fingerings.

Developing the ability to put ideas anywhere on the guitar neck is vital for mastering the art of improvisation on the guitar.

Strategy 4. Master the Fretboard.

Consider the following, for mastering the fretboard:

Since there are multiple places to play most notes and there are multiple fingers and orientations of the hand which can be used, the key to flexible fingerings is to learn to think beyond position playing. Some strategies for this include

- Learning to become comfortable with expanding and contracting the hand to facilitate position changes while playing.

- Becoming comfortable with slides and shifts.

- Knowing your note repeat points.

With any arpeggio or melodic fragment, you always have multiple options to switch strings in order to change the orientation of a given note or notes on the neck. The main reasons for doing this are:

- to facilitate a particular articulation (picking, legato, etc.).
- to facilitate movement across more or fewer strings vertically.
- to facilitate movement up or down the neck horizontally.

Practice ideas both vertically and horizontally. As discussed in chapter 2, *vertical* refers to the up and down direction in relation to the ground, and *horizontal* refers to the side to side direction in relation to the neck when it is being held in typical guitar playing position.

Vertical Strategies

Vertical strategies include:

- Picking hand articulations: What mix of alternate picking, economy picking, or no picking (legato) to use?
- Fretting hand fingerings: Which fingerings match your articulation goals and techniques?

Here is one vertical strategy for C major diatonic seventh chord arpeggios.

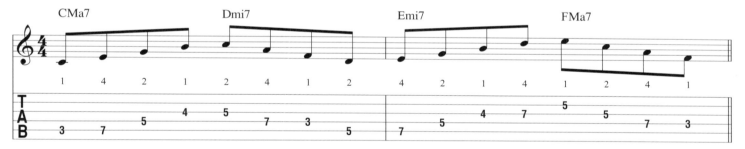

FIG. 5.1. Vertical Approach to Playing Diatonic Seventh Chord Arpeggios in C Major

Horizontal Strategies

Practice strategies for developing horizontal playing include:

- Practicing four-note cells and other structures on two adjacent strings, and moving them up and down the neck.
- Practicing them on three adjacent strings and move up and down the neck.

Arranged in figure 5.2 is a series of diatonic seventh chord arpeggios on a group of three adjacent strings. Notice that position shifts are accomplished here via shifts/slides for the first finger when ascending. So here, the first finger is the "lead" finger. In some situations, other fingers might lead.

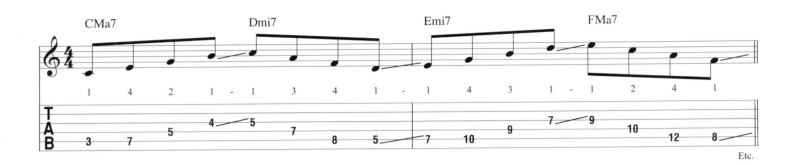

FIG. 5.2. CMa7 Performed Horizontally

Practice horizontal fingerings by contracting and expanding the hand as illustrated in figure 5.3 on a group of two adjacent strings.

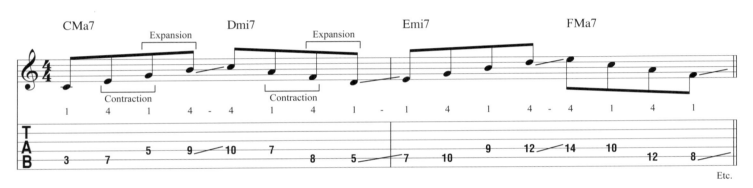

FIG. 5.3. Position Contracting and Expanding

Practice shifting between vertical and horizontal fingerings. Many of these types of fingering approaches are demonstrated in the "Perpetual Motion Etude 1" in figure 5.20.

THE PRIMORDIAL LICK

Check out this sound:

Audio 20

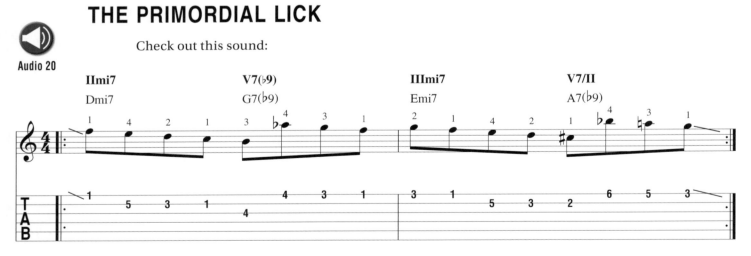

FIG. 5.4. Primordial Lick

What do you notice about the chords and the melodic material being played over it?

1. Chords

   - The harmonic pattern is common, and it works well as a *loop*—often repeated in this way, as a "turnaround" or "tag" at the end of a song form.

2. Melody

   - The melody is *one idea consisting of two four-note cells*, which are transposed (sequenced) to work over both chord pairs, each of which is a two-five.

   - It forms a *natural loop* because the last note of the phrase flows by stepwise motion into the first note.

   - It conforms to *all* the guidelines for creating effective "flow" while reflecting the underlying harmony.

   - Harmonically descriptive notes are on downbeats.

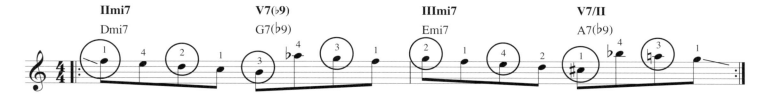

FIG. 5.5. Harmonically Descriptive Notes on Downbeats

   - The melody approaches each point of chord change by step.

FIG. 5.6. Chords Approached by Step

   - When leaps occur, they are either from CT to T or vice-versa. (The ♭9 is an available tension on dominant 7 chords.)

FIG. 5.7. Leaps from CT to T or T to CT

• It has a balance of vertical and horizontal movement.

FIG. 5.8. Vertical/Horizontal Balance

3. 3-to-7 and 7-to-3 Voice Leading

• A particularly strong harmonic movement occurs when, at the point of chord change, 3's and/or 7's move stepwise into each other. This happens to be easy to engineer when the chords are moving exclusively or primarily by cycle V root motion, as is the case here.

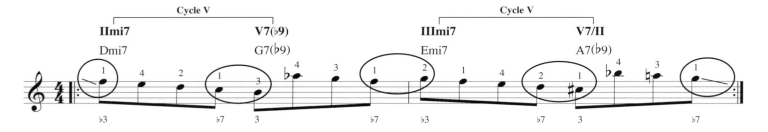

FIG. 5.9. Voice Leading of 3 and 7

You may already recognize this lick as sounding familiar. That is because it, and its underlying principles, have been used since the time of Bach, throughout the common practice period, up to Charlie Parker, John Coltrane, and on into the present day. It exemplifies effective voice leading and expresses essential harmonic movement.

Let's apply this to guitar, specifically.

The primordial lick is well suited for practicing the concepts in this book. Not only is it a good example of the guidelines listed previously, it also is a great grouping of notes to use to learn some *guitar specific ideas* about creative fingerings and liberating ways to navigate the guitar neck and tuning system.

Fingering Concept (Strategy 4): Hand Expansion and Contraction

This concept of hand expansion/contraction is one way to go beyond the traditional "one finger per fret" position approach to guitar fingerings and makes use of the left hand's ability to contract to less than a four-fret area and expand to as much as a seven-fret stretch, as a mechanism for facilitating useful movements up and down the fretboard with alternate fingerings.

The concept will be used extensively in this chapter. You'll get a sense of it by trying to play the following ideas with the fingerings I have listed for them.

Practice Strategy: Lick Looping

In taking on an ambitious task like learning to improvise over changes, less is more! (Strategy 1) One proven effective way to do this is with *lick looping*.

Lick looping is accomplished by forming groups of four-note cells (i.e., musical ideas) into "loops" that strategically link together. First, you form loops that cover multiple strings. Then, a four- or five-fret area of activity with all strings and eventually the whole neck can be covered both vertically and horizontally.

In this way, the idea *transcends fingering and doesn't limit you to one position or area of the neck.* When you know something this well, you no longer have to think about it. It becomes something you can access anytime, from any finger, *anywhere on the neck.* You do this on guitar by learning to think creatively about fingering.

Guitarists, because of the nature of their instrument, often become locked into particular fingering concepts that limit the creative flow in their playing. Since the nature of the guitar tends to encourage position playing, it's important to pay particular attention to fingering strategies that facilitate movement *across positions*, horizontally up and down the neck.

Options for rapidly and efficiently moving horizontally include:

- **Slides/Shifts:** One finger moves by sliding or shifting on the same string, to get the whole hand into a new location.

- **Collapse/Expand the Hand:** The player "closes down" the hand by bringing outer fingers close together over a few adjacent frets in order to set up a move up or down horizontally, which happens when the hand "opens up" (returns to a full four- or five-fret span) in its new location.

If we apply lick looping along with a mix of in-position and position-shifting fingering techniques, we can learn the primordial lick over the entire fingerboard and completely master it. Once you have learned myriad ways to link fingerings for one particular idea up the neck, each new lick you loop will be significantly easier to master. And with this way of practicing, by the time you're finished, you will *really* know the idea. It will be *deeply* learned and totally available to you as a foundational idea to build from.

NOTE: When two-fives are functioning diatonically, as they are here, it's common to use diatonic passing notes. So apart from the chromatic notes required for certain chord tones, and for those required for the ♭9's, all passing tones in this version of the primordial lick are diatonic.

You'll notice that the fingerings I've put on this series of notes facilitate playing the lick repeatedly in one area of the neck provided the final note (G), played with the first finger, slides/shifts down from the third fret to the first fret.

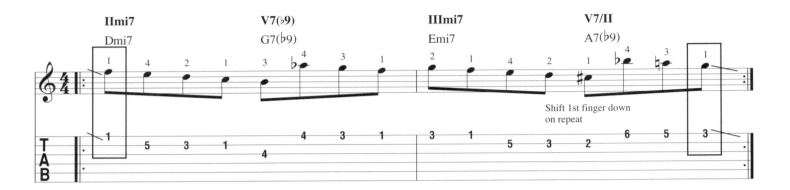

FIG. 5.10. Loop Fingering

This works well for keeping the lick looped in one, six-fret area over mostly two strings. NOTE: I'm purposely avoiding the use of open strings so that each fingering is easily movable.

This fingering can *also* work as a way to shift horizontally *up* the neck *if* that last first finger G is *not* moved down but instead becomes the new position to anchor your hand from.

Notice these fingering strategies in figure 5.11:

- **mm. 1–2: Expansion.** The finger stretch here allows for the option to move upward.

- **mm. 2–3: In Position.** Accessing F with the fourth finger on the second string (instead of moving down, as before) facilitates a move *up* the neck.

- **m. 4: Downward Shift.** A downward shift of the first finger allows us to return to the start.

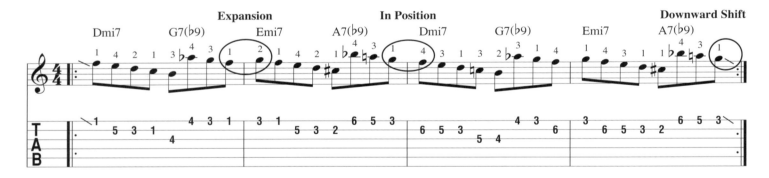

FIG. 5.11. Facilitating Moves Up the Neck

The lick loop has now been expanded from two measures to four measures. We have used "hand expansion" (stretching) in the transition from measure 1 to measure 2, and shifts in measure 4, to allow us to cover more neck area. As written in figure 5.11, we can also still move the idea down to the original location by shifting down with the first finger on the last note as before.

This process can potentially cover the whole neck. You can see that by expanding our "loop" with flexible fingerings, we have a strategy that eventually will allow us to move the idea up and down the entire fingerboard. Using a limited number of strings is advisable in the beginning so that there are fewer fingerings to learn.

The fingering here is not the only way to accomplish this. Though we will continue to need to "expand" the hand, or shift, to facilitate a move to a higher place on the neck, there are other points where this could be done and other locations in the series of notes to execute the upward move. Here are some guidelines for other possible fingerings:

1. When expanding (stretching), it's usually most practical to do so between fingers 1 and 2, or 1 and 4. On higher frets, which are closer together, sometimes stretches between fingers 3 and 4 can work.

2. When shifting, you can potentially use any finger, but make sure the fingering surrounding the shift is comfortable for the hand and works well with subsequent notes.

3. Too many shifts in a row can make it difficult to control articulation and achieve speed.

The fingerings shown here employ hand expansion/contraction and/or slides/ shifts in ways that I prefer, but they do not represent every possibility. Particular fingering solutions may vary, but it's the *concept* of finding ergonomic fingerings that allows us to move around the neck that is most important to keep top of mind. You are encouraged to experiment with different fingerings to find ways that work best for you with any given selection of notes. What is crucial is that you *learn multiple ways to play each idea* so that you can be flexible and the idea itself can be portable on the instrument.

Next let's look at some ways to facilitate upward and downward looping with some connecting material.

Horizontal Movement: One example of fingering a single idea to cover the entire neck horizontally.

The exercise in figure 5.12 shows the primordial lick fingered to facilitate a gradual movement all the way up and down the neck. It occupies mostly a three-string group the whole time, shifting from higher strings to lower strings as it moves up the neck, then the reverse as the lick moves back down. At any point, with minor adaptations, the lick could be looped in the same area of activity.

FIG. 5.12. Primordial Lick Up and Down the Neck

Vertical Movement: Adding Ways to Change Octaves

Since we're trying to maintain stepwise motion as we transition from the end of one four-note cell to another, we need a way to change octaves gradually, without leaps at the point of chord change. We can accomplish this by doing one or both of the following:

1. **Octave Transpose.** With this lick, transposing between the 3 and the ♭9 on the dominant 7 chord on the "and" of beat 3 works particularly well. (Notice the change in fingerings required to make this ergonomic.) Changing the octaves between the 3 and ♭9 allows us to move vertically.

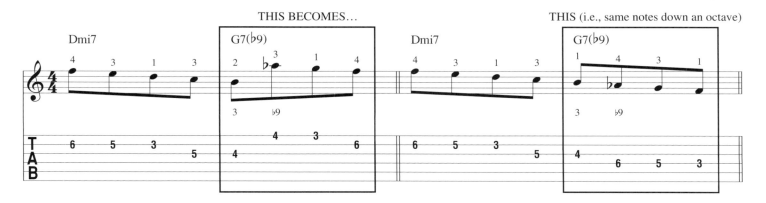

FIG. 5.13. How to Octave Transpose

Applied to the whole four-chord lick, you could end up with this. Next, you'll need to go to low F in order to have stepwise transition.

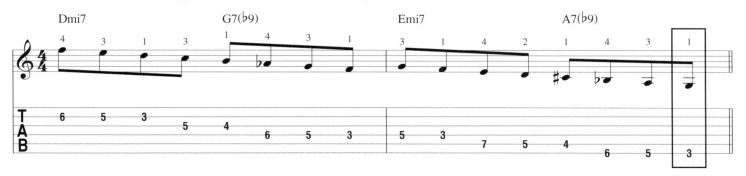

FIG. 5.14. Octave Shifts

2. **Use "Scale Cells."** This allows us to "walk stepwise" down or up octaves. At any point, you can also revert to going *up* from 3 to ♭9 instead of down to keep the lick in a playable area. For example, you could play the previous two measures but go up the octave on the A7(♭9) to "position" a starting point for a repeat in a higher note range.

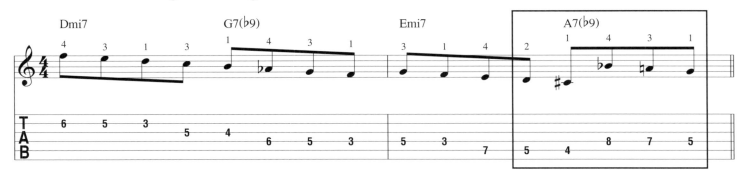

FIG. 5.15. Going Up to Stay in a Playable Area

However, if you do find yourself in an extreme area of the neck (very low or very high), or for any reason, you want to work your way up or down, another option is to use a *scale cell*.

HOW TO USE SCALE CELLS

A *scale cell* is a four-note passage that moves entirely stepwise through the scale of the moment, either up or down. It's common to use diatonic notes on diatonic chords and also on secondary dominants (because diatonic notes always work well with, and are contained in, the basic secondary dominant chord scales). As shown in figure 5.16, if we had octave-transposed down 3 to ♭9 twice in a row, we would find ourselves at a low F upon resolution to the Dmi7 chord (if we want to retain stepwise movement at point of chord change). You'll need to go to low F in order to have a stepwise transition.

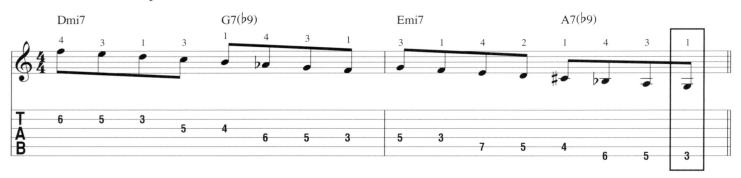

FIG. 5.16. 3 and ♭9 Leading to Low F

In a situation like this, we can keep going by octave transposing from ♭3 to 9 on the Dmi7 chord like this:

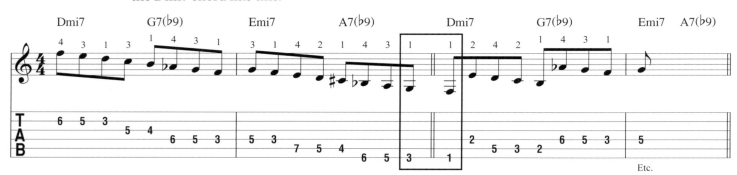

FIG. 5.17. Transposing After F

However, using scale cells gives us a pleasing alternative—one that allows for some horizontal texture and some very ergonomic fingering options.

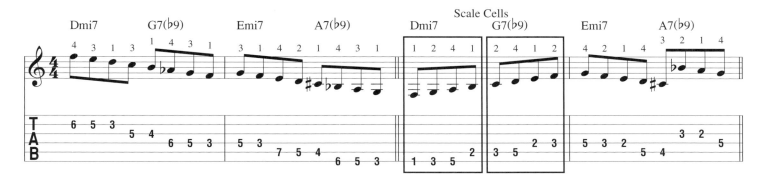

FIG. 5.18. Using Scale Cells

Directional scalar movement is a useful element to add to our lick-looping tool box. It allows for free movement through octaves and gives us another option for changing position. The only issue is that occasionally, as happens in this case, a harmonic avoid note (HAN) can end up on a downbeat. Here, it's the C on beat 3. Later, we'll learn about inserting chromatics or using the bebop scale to remedy this kind of situation, but the fact is, in common practice, this exception is used often and seems to not detract from the effectiveness of the line when a harmonic avoid note is part of an upward or downward gesture. The directional nature of the line "points" to the ultimate target so strongly that we can tolerate the passing dissonance.

As a quick passing dissonance within a directional line, S4 can be okay, particularly at moderate to faster tempos.

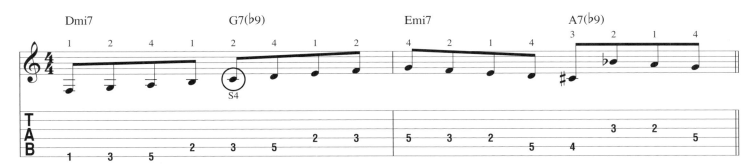

FIG. 5.19. Harmonic Avoid Note C (S4)

Now that we have added the options of octave transposition and scale cell use, we can cover the fingerboard with lick looping much more easily and with more variety of sound.

PERPETUAL MOTION ETUDE 1

This etude combines strategies 1 and 4: "Less Is More" and "Flexible Fingerings." It is designed to show some possible pathways to cover the entire neck with the primordial lick integrated with scale cells.

In this exercise, we are moving both vertically and horizontally around the neck while using a combo of the original form of the idea, the octave transposed version, and scale cells up and down. Note that we end up playing the ideas from different starting fingers, which is crucial to developing creative freedom with flexible fingerings. It covers the entire fingerboard via a series of loops and transitions.

To develop your own ability to play the same idea in many places on the neck, remember that notes on the guitar are repeated every five frets between adjacent strings (four frets between strings 3 and 2). Being constantly aware of those repeat points helps you develop your own ability to creatively generate alternative fingerings.

Notice the use of all strings in an area before each shift to a new area. This is done in order to fully explore a range of ways to access the notes. Fingerings are designed to illustrate flexible transitional fingering strategies. Replay or loop the accompanying audio track as needed. NOTE: Audio track ends after transition 7.

Audio 21–22

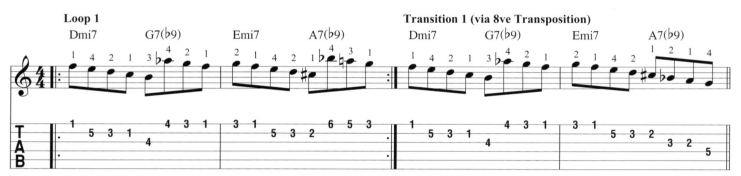

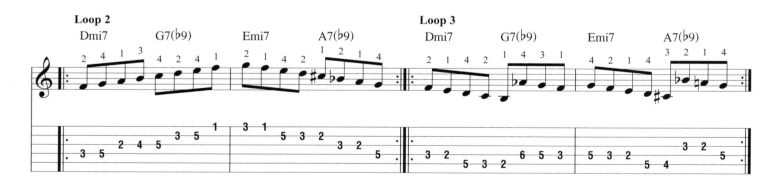

FIG. 5.20. Perpetual Motion Etude 1

Though further upward motion is possible, we now will reverse direction to show some fingering strategies for navigation *downward* along the neck.

Unlike our upward journey, which was engineered to take our time fully covering the neck both vertically and horizontally, the fingerings in figure 5.21 are designed for constant position shifts downward, and thus sacrifice some of the possible vertical movement. Fingerings designed to get quickly from one part of the neck to another horizontally can be worked out for either upward or downward direction, of course; here we are focusing on downward direction. This is accomplished by *integrating transitional fingerings into the looping process.*

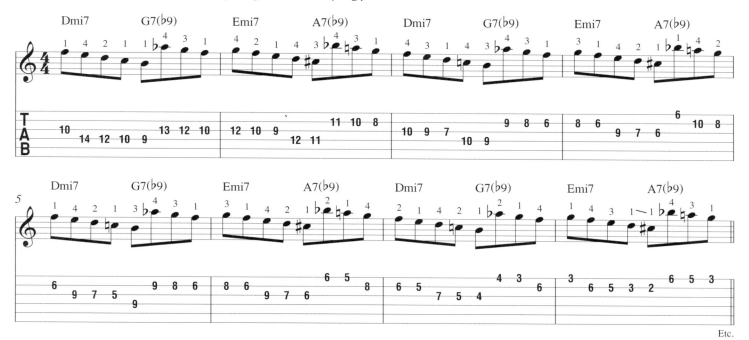

FIG. 5.21. Heading Downward

It is *highly recommended* that you learn the preceding etude (with the fingerings shown) before moving on because this study *exemplifies the essential strategy* at the heart of this method—namely, *less is more!* Strategy 1.

Learning a *few* effective and powerful licks *thoroughly*, over the entire neck, will lead to faster progress, and ultimately, more vocabulary and creative freedom. Once you can play it, you'll be internally "hearing" the changes and voice-leading well.

Next, internalize the material further by using these same cells in different ways "on the fly." This is much like sight-reading notation but with only a few phrases... and you won't be reading them but remembering them while visualizing/audiating the possible variations. In other words, the number of phrases is still limited, but you can introduce some creative use of them by improvising different ways to fit them together on the spur of the moment.

This can be practiced as a sort of game in which you can adjust the rules to get the appropriate amount of challenge. Some challenges could be:

1. Play in one loop three times maximum, then make at least one change, such as octave transposition or scale cell up/down to another loop location.

2. Play two times only before changing it.

3. Play a figure only once before moving it. This will result in constant movement and is very challenging.

4. Using a combination of cells, you must touch every string at least once before shifting your main area of activity up or down the neck.

Mastery Measurements Strategy

You are ready to move on when you can do the following:

1. Play "Perpetual Motion Etude 1" in a steady, slow/moderate tempo (♩ = 85 or so) using either the indicated fingerings or alternatives that you have thoughtfully developed to facilitate efficient movement.

2. In constant eighth notes and in tempo, play your own improvised version of the etude while navigating your way up and down the neck utilizing only:

   - the two original four-note cells

   - the 3 to ♭9 octave transposition variation

   - diatonic scale cells

3. Play any of the components in step 2 beginning on any finger (1, 2, 3, 4). This is exemplified in the etude.

Next Step: Continue to explore and apply 3-to-7 and 7-to-3 motion by learning more four-note cells that use this voice leading.

Once you can move freely around the neck with the primordial lick, you have set the stage for a steady building of vocabulary and fluency.

The most efficient way to do this is to build on what you know. You know that 3 to 7 and 7 to 3 works well, and you have a lot of fingerings at your disposal that are related to these voice leading motions. The next step is to choose from a group of new four-note cells that also move 3 to 7 or 7 to 3, and substitute one new four-note cell at a time as you continue to apply the "cover the entire neck" approach.

To get you started, here are some additional patterns that utilize 3 to 7/7 to 3.

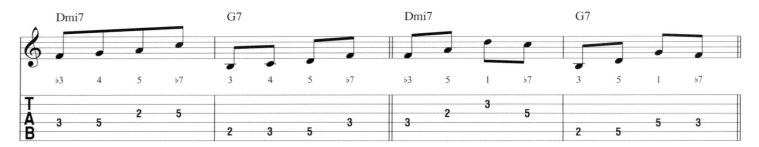

FIG. 5.22. Four-Note Cells that Move from 3 to 7 or 7 to 3

In order to build vocabulary in a manageable way, change only one four-note cell at a time. *Integrate the new four-note cell with one that you already know well.*

As an illustration, let's apply this to our IImi7 V7 IIImi7 V7/II turnaround (Dmi7 G7 Emi7 A7). In figure 5.23, a new 3, 4, 5, 7 cell is paired to the related mi7 chords, but the original four-note cell remains on the dominant seventh chords:

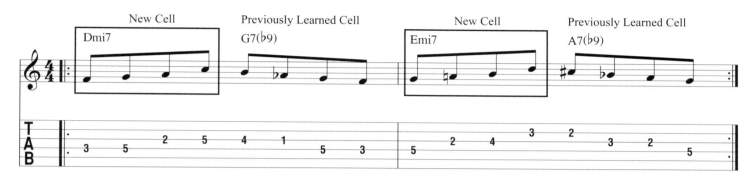

FIG. 5.23. Integrating a New Cell

The result is a new loop that you can then learn to move over the entire neck, using your growing knowledge of the fretboard and flexible fingering options.

Next, try switching this process. This time, keep the original scale cell on the mi7 chords and apply a new cell (3, 5, 1, 7) on the dominant 7 chords.

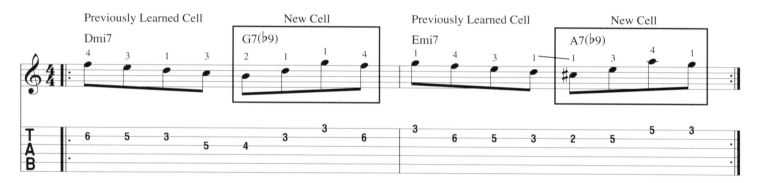

FIG. 5.24. New Cell on Dominant 7 Chords

Gradually substituting new material, integrated with previously learned material, yields the most effective, quickest learning of new vocabulary. This approach works well with all of the five strategies.

One of the most important things to learn is how to use practice time most effectively. The five strategies in this book all help you do that.

PRACTICING 15 MINUTES AT A TIME

New loops such as the ones presented earlier in this chapter can be mastered in 15 minutes of practice time (or less). Thus, they represent a good model for how to use practice time in an efficient and sustainable way. The strategy is to structure your practice by coming up with short-term goals, achievable in 15 minutes or less (strategy 2).

These 15 minute goals allow you to make progress every day, even on days when you only have 15 minutes to practice! Set goals that are *achievable meaningfully* and that are *measurable* (strategy 3) in 15 minutes or less, and you'll *know* that you are making progress. That knowledge will support your momentum, positive attitude, and sense of achievement.

An example of a 15 minute goal would be: "I am going to pair one new 3-to-7 four-note cell with one that I already know, and learn to play one fingering of the new loop I create." The previous two examples demonstrate something along those lines.

Also remember to link your goal to a mastery measurement (strategy 3):

Goal: *"I'm going to work on playing this new loop smoothly until I can play it cleanly in tempo three times correctly with a metronome at ____ tempo."*

Then the next time you practice, you could review that previously created loop, measure it and if there's time, work out a new 15 minute goal related to it. The new 15 minute goal could be anything that builds logically on the first goal.

For example, a next, related goal might be to focus on expanding the area over which you can play your new loop:

Goal: *"Create one new location for the loop with octave transposition, a scale cell, or both."*

In this way, you can experience a sense of accomplishment and momentum every 15 minutes, as you progress on a journey that will take many hours to complete.

Here is a suggested practice routine based on this idea. Bear in mind that review and consolidation are necessary, so sometimes, your 15 minute goal might be to simply review and consolidate something achieved in a 15 minute goal the previous day.

15 MINUTE GOAL EXAMPLE PRACTICE ROUTINE
Learn one loop with good, playable fingering.
Create a new loop nearby (vertical or horizontal) with good fingerings.
Create a well fingered transition from loop 1 to loop 2.
Review/consolidate previously learned loops.
Repeat this process until you can move the loop horizontally and vertically over the entire fingerboard in a steady tempo.
Replace one previously learned four-note cell with a new one.
Repeat the process until the new loop is playable over the entire neck.

MORE 3-TO-7 LOOP MATERIAL APPLIED MORE WIDELY

Continued progress requires that you keep learning and integrating additional four-note cells into your vocabulary. It also requires that you learn to apply your loops in a wider variety of situations. Transposing melodic ideas to different keys is the most obvious expansion of application.

Application to different kinds of progressions is another way to get more use out of what you learn. So far, we have mainly used the Dmi7 G7 Emi7 A7 harmonic loop. But the concepts learned can be applied to many other progressions. The most obvious is the ubiquitous IImi7 V7 to IMa7 (or mi7) progression.

Here are a few examples showing one unvaried cell (on the related II chord) with a varied cell (on the V7) resolving to the 3 (or ♭3) of a major or minor "I" chord.

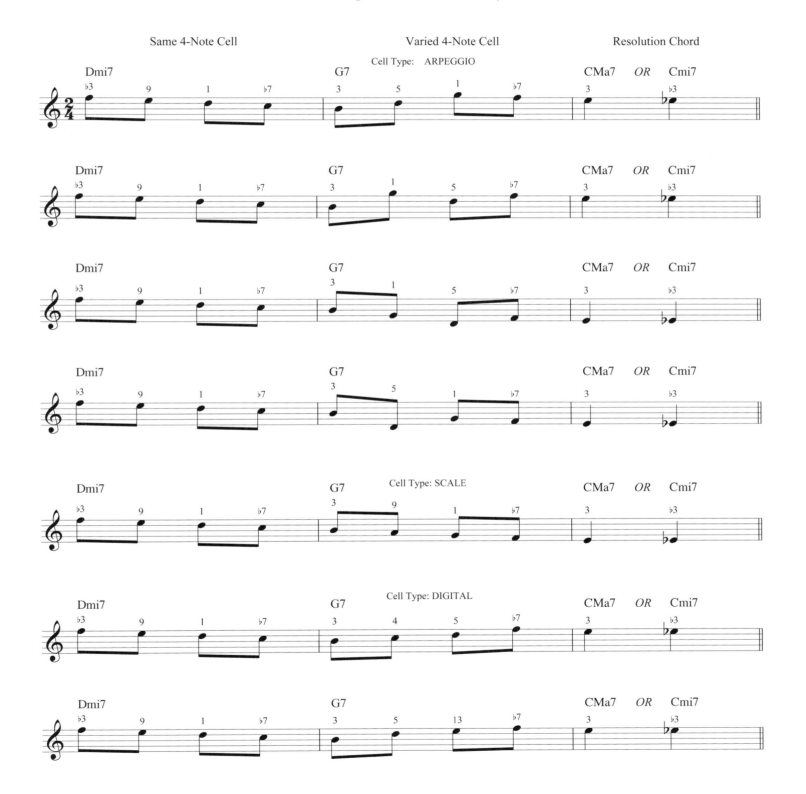

FIG. 5.25. Combining Varied and Unvaried Cells

Next is the same idea but with the variation applied to the IImi7 chord while keeping the V7 four-note cell unchanged.

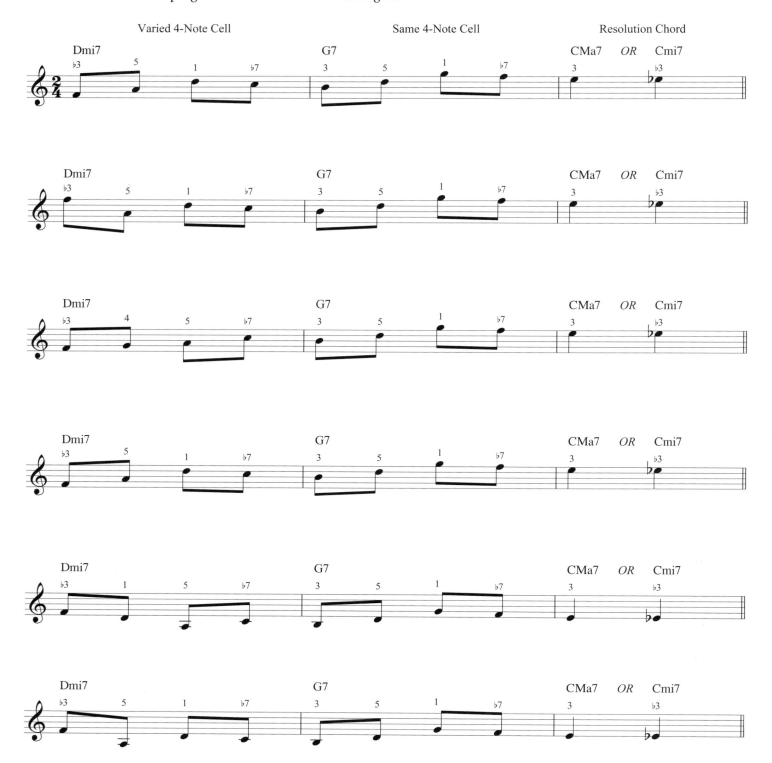

FIG. 5.26. Beginning with a Varied Cell

PERPETUAL MOTION ETUDE 2

In "Perpetual Motion Etude 2," there are a wider variety of four-note cells, still using the 3 to 7/7 to 3 concept. It incorporates lick looping, octave transposition, and scale cells, arranged to apply new material to multiple string sets and areas of the neck. Replay or loop the accompanying audio track as needed.

Audio 23

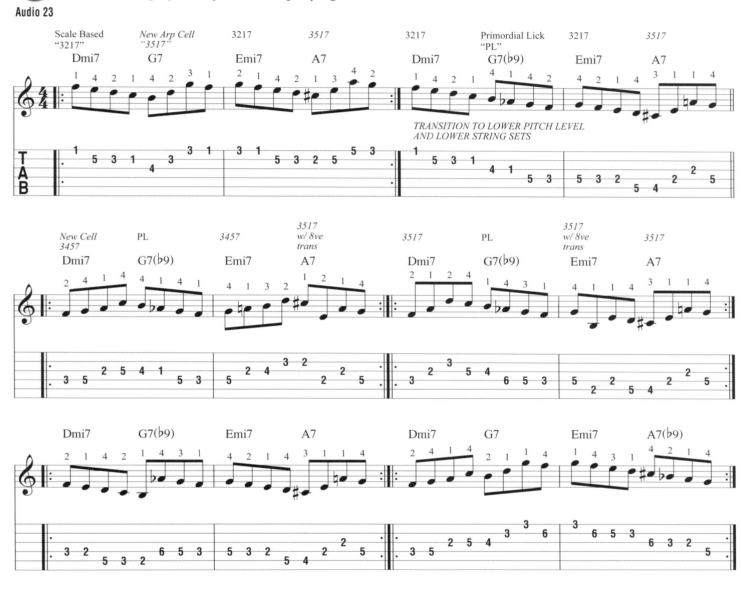

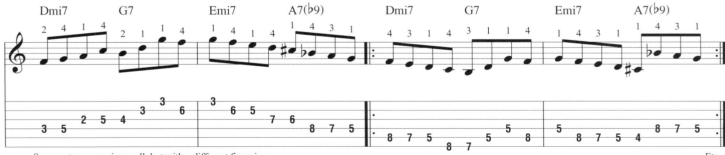

Same notes as previous cell, but with a different fingering
that allows for a *transitional* passage, moving *up* the neck.

Etc.

FIG. 5.27. Perpetual Motion Etude 2

At any point, you can make this kind of choice:

FIG. 5.28. Decision Point

This etude is intentionally less comprehensive than "Perpetual Motion Etude 1." It is designed for you to continue it. In the last few measures, its annotations indicate your ever-present choices: at any point, you can either stay in an area to establish a loop and learn a new fingering thoroughly or you can use flexible fingerings via expansion/contraction of the hand (or slides) to move higher or lower on the neck to create a loop in a new area.

You are encouraged to work with these principles until you can improvise, in real time, *the order and voice leading of 3-to-7 and 7-to-3 four-note cells*, while simultaneously using shifts and flexible fingerings to cover the entire neck *without having to stop playing*. Once you can do this with a given set of four-note cells, you will be able to "pre hear" the cells extremely well and reliably execute them anywhere on the neck in real improvisational settings—not only as memorized licks, but as springboards for further, more spontaneous improvisational ideas.

CHAPTER 6

More Resources for Navigating the Changes

Ideas based on 3 to 7/7 to 3 are a great foundation, but in order to begin to internalize a wider variety of vocabulary, we need to move beyond this one concept. As laid out in chapter 5, the guidelines encourage stepwise movement at the point of chord change *to any available note*, not just 3 or 7. They also allow for leaping at point of chord change, as long as the leap is from one available note to another. Usually, the leap is followed by a stepwise move in the opposite direction.

And finally, our guidelines allow for emphasis (placement on a downbeat) of "harmonic avoid notes," as long as the note is treated like a suspension that resolves to an available note immediately subsequent, and/or if it is a "blues" note (see later in this chapter).

With all these new possibilities, the sky is the limit! In order to avoid presenting an overwhelming number of options, the following list narrows things down, focusing on some of the more common four-note cells from the bebop and blues musical languages. Each cell is labeled with the category it is derived from (e.g., arpeggio, scale, approach note, etc.) and illustrated with a short musical example.

Later in the book, all of these cells (plus a few more) will be used in constant note value solos that use the guidelines applied to the common chord progressions we explored earlier.

These examples are a select group. You are encouraged to explore the great multitude of potential patterns that can be derived from these concepts.

FOUR-NOTE CELL CONCEPTS

Commonly used four-note cells can be derived from the following categories.

1. Scale-Based Patterns

   - **Any grouping of four consecutive notes from the chord scale**, going up or down.

Audio 24

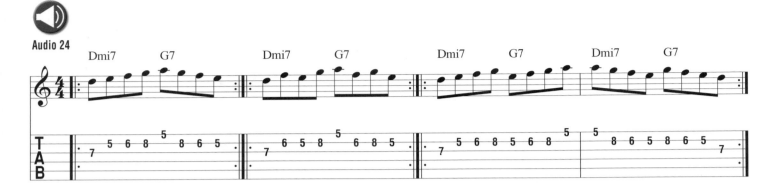

FIG. 6.1. Scale-Based Patterns

Audio 25

- **Sequencing in Thirds.** Up or down.

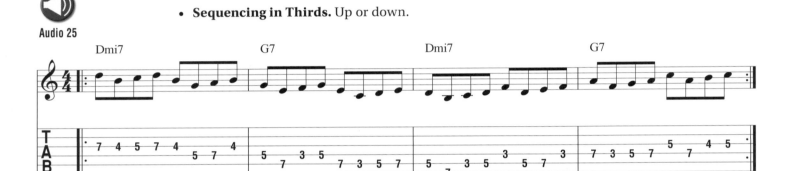

FIG. 6.2. Sequencing in Thirds

Audio 26

- **Scales with Integrated Chromatics/Half Steps.** Here, the pattern is scale down/scale down/chromatic up.

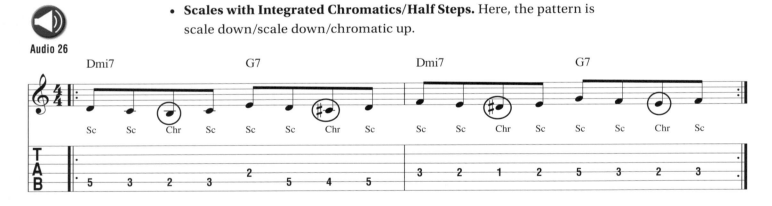

FIG. 6.3. Scale with Integrated Chromatics

- **Scale-Based "Digital" or "Number" Patterns.** These ideas are transposable to different starting points—any "available" notes of the chord scale. What's important is the general shape/gesture. Here's a "shape" expressed as "1231."

FIG. 6.4. Scale-Based Digital Pattern

In figure 6.5, the previous digital pattern is arranged and transposed to create stepwise transitions between chords.

FIG. 6.5. Variation of Figure 6.4 with Stepwise Transitions between Chords

- **Another Common Digital Pattern:** 1235 and its various transpositions.

FIG. 6.6. Digital Pattern 1235 Transposed to 3457

Audio 27

The 1235 pattern arranged to create stepwise transitions:

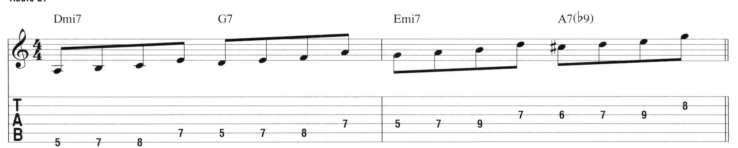

FIG. 6.7. Variation of 1235 Pattern with Stepwise Transitions

2. Arpeggio-Based Patterns

- *"Inside" arpeggio patterns* are any four-note patterns that use exclusively chord tones. In a seventh chord, this would be 1357, in any order. Here are a few common ones:

FIG. 6.8. Inside Arpeggio Patterns

Here are some combinations of the previous example featuring stepwise movement at point of chord change and some octave transpositions, represented here as a series of loops.

Audio 28

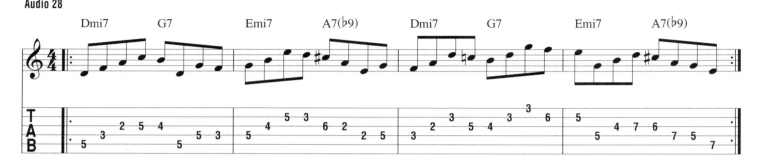

FIG. 6.9. Inside Arpeggio Variations

- **Seventh Chord Superimpositions.** As mentioned in an earlier chapter, it's common and useful to superimpose seventh chords built on various chord tones as one way to feature tensions in your improvised lines. The potential seventh chord super-impositions are ones from the 3, 5, and 7 of the original chord. The tensions they yield are listed below.

Superimpose a 7th chord built on original chord's **3rd** to get 3, 5, 7, 9 *"3 gives you 9"*	Superimpose a 7th chord built on original chord's **5th** to get 5, 7, 9, 11 *"5 gives you 11"*	Superimpose a 7th chord built on original chord's **7th** to get 7, 9, 11, 13 *"7 gives you 13"*

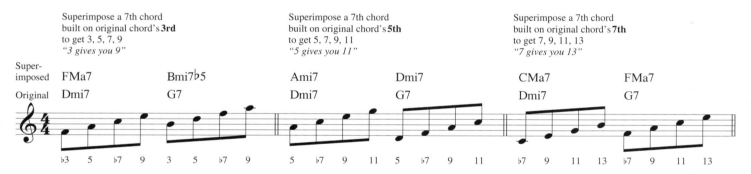

FIG. 6.10. Superimposed Seventh Chords

Audio 29

Below are some superimposed arpeggios using voice leading and octave transpositions arranged in a series of loops.

FIG. 6.11. Variations of Seventh Chord Superimpositions

- **Arpeggio-Based Patterns with Additional Chromatics (embellished arpeggios).** This category consists of four-note cells in which three out of four notes are from the arpeggio, or upper extension, and one note is an approach tone. In the example below the approach tone is a chromatic approach from below and is on the downbeat and thus is an "accented" approach note. . . a dissonance placed intentionally on a downbeat which is then immediately resolved.

Audio 30

FIG. 6.12. Arpeggio-Based Patterns with Chromatics

3. Approach-Note Based Patterns

- Approach notes (typically placed on the "and"/upbeat) are used to lead the ear to a target note—typically a chord tone or available tension on a downbeat. Approach note patterns can be one note or a group of notes. The notes can be diatonic, chromatic, or a combination of both. Here are the common types: (NOTE: *Chromatic motion* is a half step away from the target note. Sometimes, *scale notes* are also a half step away from the target, and the context will dictate how you describe the motion.)

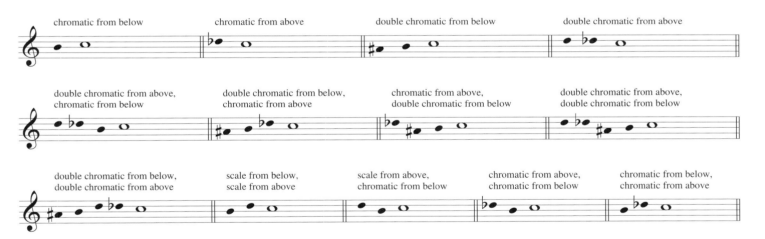

FIG. 6.13. Approach Note Patterns

Here are some common applications of approach notes arranged in four-note cells applied to chords:

- **Double Chromatic** from above and below.

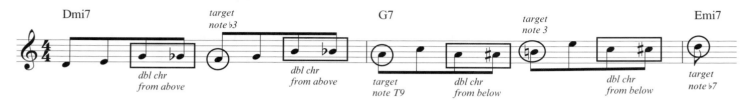

FIG. 6.14. Double Chromatic Approach

- **Double Chromatic/Scale Combo** as a three-note approach tone pattern.

Audio 31

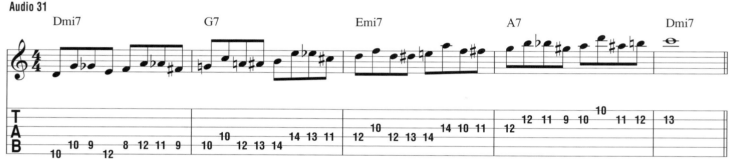

FIG. 6.15. Double Chromatic/Scale Combo

4. Dominant "Altered" Cells

- Dominant chords often work well with added "altered" tensions ♭9, #9, #11, ♭13. These notes add intensity and additional dissonance to the already inherently restless sound of dominant chords.

Listen carefully to the following two versions of the same two-five lick. The first uses diatonic notes and tensions; the second uses altered tensions. Notice the darker sound of the altered version.

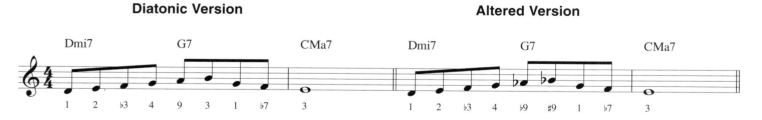

FIG. 6.16. Diatonic and Altered Tensions

NOTE: In figure 6.16, the note B♭ played against the G7 is labeled "#9" because that is the way it is functioning aurally. It is heard as #9 whether it's spelled as "A#" or "B♭."

Audio 32

Below are a few common "altered" four-note cells that work well against dominant chords. I'm representing them here in the context of a II V I phrase with stepwise voice leading at chord change.

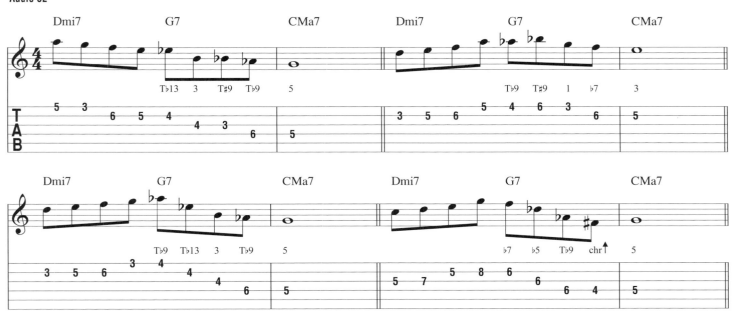

FIG. 6.17. Altered Four-Note Cells on Dominant 7 Chords

5. Chromatic "Connector" Cells

- Check out the sound of figure 6.18 (track 33). The first measure and the second measure sound quite different but both "work" over the changes. The first measure uses two four-note cells that are in the "chromatic cell" category; the second measure should be recognizable as the "primordial lick" using ♭9 on the G7.

Audio 33

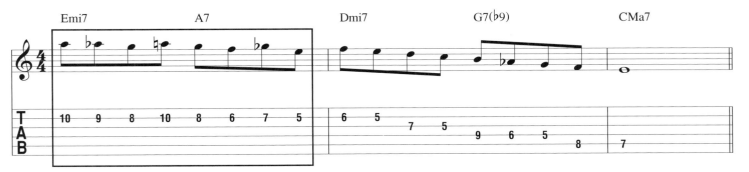

FIG. 6.18. Chromatic Connector Cells

Improvisers often use chromatic "connector" cells as a way to "float" over the changes and/or as a way to get from point A to point B with a chromatic texture.

The "floating" effect comes from the fact that the idea is not necessarily fully descriptive of the chord underneath but works more as a melodic "gesture" leading the listener's ear in a particular direction and helping the idea sound ordered even if some of the notes could be analyzed as "wrong" notes over the chord of the moment.

The directional nature of the cell is more powerful than any passing dissonance. An easy to understand application of this concept is a glissando. The particular notes in a glissando are not as important as the gesture upward or downward. In a chromatic cell, the notes are important, but the strength of the gesture—if properly resolved at the end—is ultimately what makes it work.

In other words, if a chromatic pattern or gesture is strong and played with authority, and if the tempo relationships support it (not too slow), an improviser can potentially play any note over any chord as long as the idea is resolved in a convincing way on a strong beat.

Here are some common, useful chromatic connector/gesture cells:

- **Whole step cell.** Use anywhere that you want to emphasize two notes a whole step apart.

Audio 34

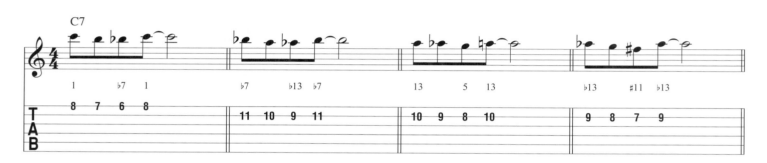

FIG. 6.19. Whole Step Cell

- **Miles' Snake.** This pattern slithers downwards. It was used frequently by Miles Davis; down a whole step/up a half step/down a half step. It links two notes a minor third apart.

Audio 35

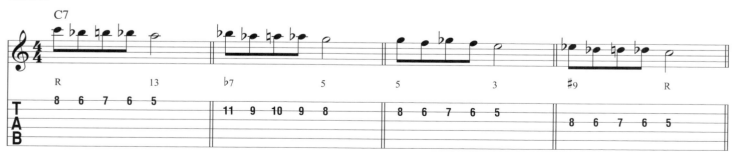

FIG. 6.20. Miles' Snake

Audio 36

- **The Chromatic Crawl.** This spans a minor third but links two notes a half step apart—chromatic from below, double chromatic from above/ chromatic from below. Use as an approach pattern to a target note.

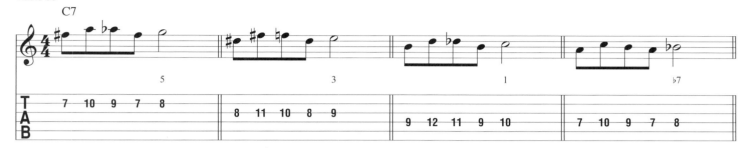

FIG. 6.21. Chromatic Crawl

It could also be used as a way to move chromatically up or down.

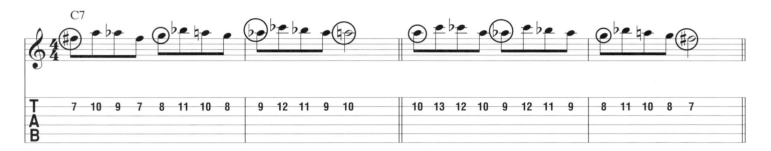

FIG. 6.22. Chromatic Crawl Up/Down

Audio 37

- **Outside In.** These cells span a major third while linking two notes a minor third apart: down a major third/up a minor third/down a minor third/up half step.

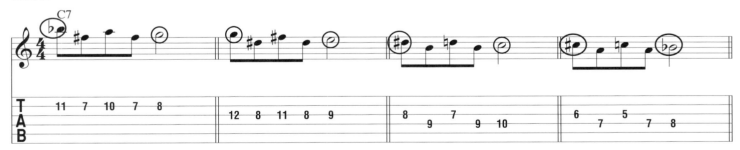

FIG. 6.23. Outside In

Audio 38

- **Whole/Half Crawl.** This spans a major second (up or down). It is used to move chromatically up or down in half steps.

FIG. 6.24. Whole/Half Crawl

- **Combinations.** Typically, these chromatic connectors are used in combination, to create variety. The following could be played over a series of chord changes but also has enough variety to work over a one chord vamp.

Audio 39

FIG. 6.25. Combining Chromatic Connectors

6. Bebop Scale Based Cells

- The bebop scale is really an approach-note concept that can be added to any seven-note scale. It is a way to turn conventional seven-note scales into eight-note scales, thus making them ideal for constant eighth note vocabulary. The concept grew out of the bebop era jazz improviser's vocabulary and has become an important resource in jazz improvisation since.

Here's how it works. When playing a series of stepwise eighth notes using seven-note scales, sometimes the notes that are featured on the downbeats can end up being harmonic avoid notes, as in the example below where S4 (F) occurs on beat 1.

FIG. 6.26. S4 on Beat 1

This situation can be remedied by simply adding a well-chosen chromatic note on an "and" (upbeat). On major 7 chords, this kind of passing tone is most often placed between scale degrees 5 and 6, thus adding a #5 to the major scale ascending, and the same note (spelled as a ♭6) to the scale descending, like this.

FIG. 6.27. Bebop Scale: Adding #5 or ♭6

Adding this chromatic note to the stepwise pattern lets you end with chord tones on all downbeats. In fact, if you start on any chord tone and use this scale with stepwise motion, every downbeat will automatically be a chord tone! This is still true even if you change direction in the middle of the line.

Adding a well-positioned chromatic passing tone to make a seven-note scale into an eight-note scale can be applied to any seven-note chord scale, and it will work the same way. The location of the added note can vary, but the most common places for it are:

- On chords with a major 6 or 7, add chromatic passing tone between scale degrees 5 and 6.

- On chords with a minor 7 (♭7), add chromatic passing tone between scale degrees 1 and ♭7.

This practice helps facilitate fluent eighth-note lines, with added color from passing chromatics, while avoiding "wrong" (HAN) notes on downbeats. It makes lines sound more "jazzy."

- **Bebop Scale Concept Applied to Four-Note Cells.** The bebop scale formula is most often applied during longer passages on a single chord (as in the bridge on "Rhythm Changes"). In the context of four-note cells, it can best be applied with the following way:

  - **Chromatic Connector Concept (CCC).** Insert one chromatic note, on an upbeat, into an otherwise pure four-note consecutive stepwise scale grouping, in order to arrive on a desired note at the end of the four-note group.

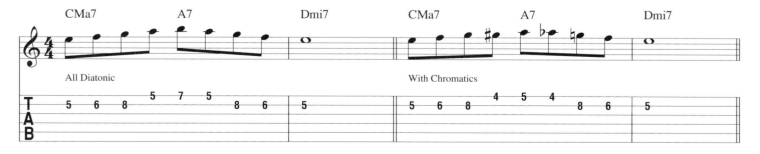

FIG. 6.28. Chromatic Connectors

CCC is a more flexible way to use the bebop scale concept. Simply insert a half-step approach, either from above or below the target note, in order to facilitate a smooth stepwise arrival at that note on a downbeat.

○ **Combo CCC/Bebop Scale.** Here's an example that uses both the bebop scale and CCC. Using both yields the most flexibility.

Audio 40

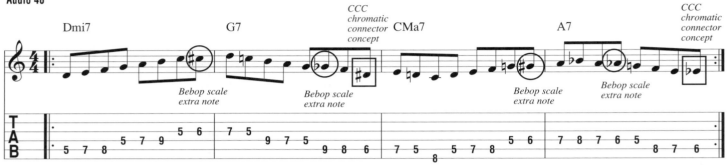

FIG. 6.29. Combining CCC and Bebop Scale

7. Blues Vocabulary Based Cells

- The blues language is hugely influential. Blues inflection can be heard in hit pop songs, chart topping country music, and R&B, as well as in rock and jazz. Any study of building useful jazz vocabulary needs to include blues elements in the mix.

For reasons of brevity, this book will focus on blues vocabulary as it relates to *note choice.* This will allow us to incorporate blues tinged material into our four-note cell learning model. But it's important to be aware that the blues language is so much more than note choice. Authenticity in any genre requires a comprehensive learning approach and a lot of deep listening. In any genre, *how* you play something is just as important to a style as *what* you play and that is certainly true of the blues.

Below are some basic resources for blues vocabulary note choice. Practicing them will help you bring "bluesy" sounds into your four-note cells and your impro-vised lines.

The primary notes which help characterize the blues sound, against either a minor or major based chord are ♭3, ♭5, ♭7.

- Blues Scale Resources:

  ○ **Tonic minor pentatonic scale.** This five-note scale includes ♭3 and ♭7.

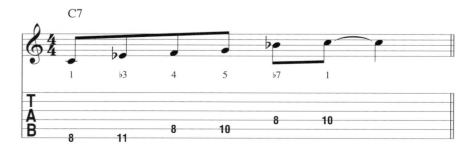

FIG. 6.30. Tonic Minor Pentatonic

○　This six-note scale adds the ♭5.

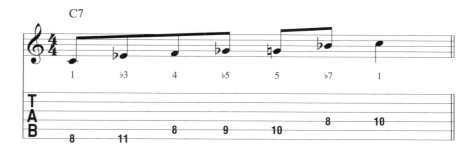

FIG. 6.31. Minor Blues Hexatonic Scale

For a very basic blues soloing approach, you could use *only* the notes from one of these scales (based on the tonic of the key). In other words, in a three-chord blues in the key of C you could use *only* the C hexatonic blues scale notes (C, E♭, F, G♭, G, B♭) as you improvise over all the chords (C7, F7, G7).

While this approach can be a good strategy for beginners, constraining yourself to only this group of notes is too limiting for full expression and doesn't allow the player enough choices to reflect all the harmonic changes, especially those in more elaborate blues progressions. Effective, creative, and nuanced blues vocabulary goes beyond the notes of the hexatonic blues scale.

For example, the minor blues scale doesn't include a major third, yet this note is used extremely commonly in the blues, over major triads and dominant 7 chords. Other interesting scale and chord tone colors are missing too.

- **Adding more notes and color to the blues.** The following additional scale and arpeggio resources enable more melodic and harmonic *variety* as you incorporate blues sounds into your improvisations. I recommend getting acquainted with them one by one (even though they can add up into one big seven-note scale in the end). Practicing them individually over cycle V and basic blues progressions (with fingerings spanning the entire fretboard) will help you learn the sound of each so that you can ultimately control which sound colors you want to highlight in your improvised, blues-inflected lines.

  ○　**Major Blues Pentatonic:** 1, ♭3, 3, 5, 6

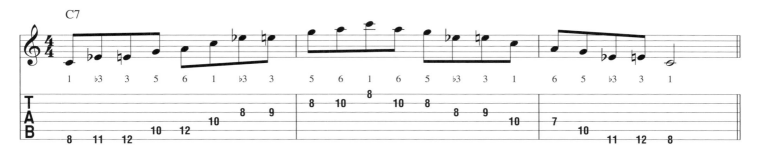

FIG. 6.32. Major Blues Pentatonic

Audio 41

Here's an eighth-note based lick using this scale exclusively.

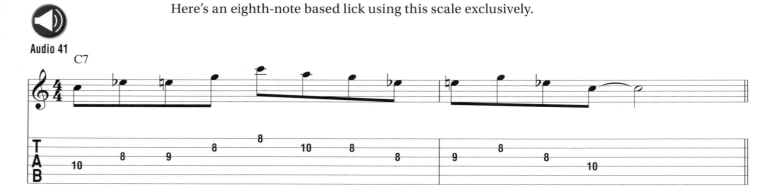

FIG. 6.33. Major Blues Pentatonic Lick

o   **Major Blues Hexatonic:** 1, 2, ♭3, 3, 5, 6. These are the same notes as the relative "minor blues hexatonic." That is, the A minor blues hexatonic consists of the same notes as C major blues hexatonic, just in a different note order.

FIG. 6.34. Major Blues Hexatonic

Audio 42

Here's a solo passage using this scale exclusively.

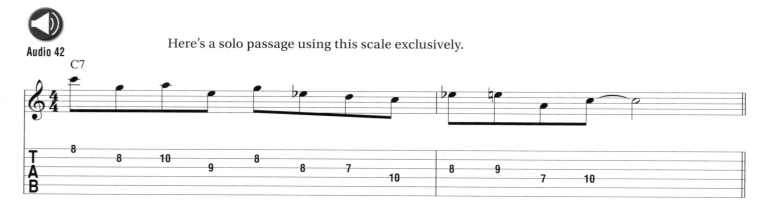

FIG. 6.35. Major Blues Hexatonic Lick

○ **Major Blues Septatonic:** 1, 2, ♭3, 3, 5, 6, ♭7. Another way to think of this is as a major pentatonic (1, 2, 3, 5, 6) with added ♭3 and ♭7.

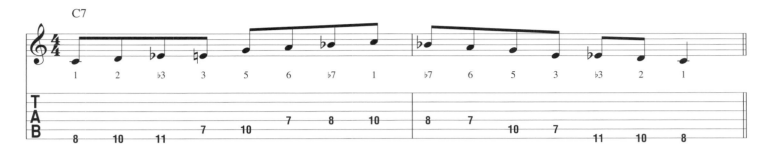

FIG. 6.36. Major Blues Septatonic

Audio 43

Here is a lick using blues septatonic exclusively, based on a constant note value, but this time, triplet eighth notes.

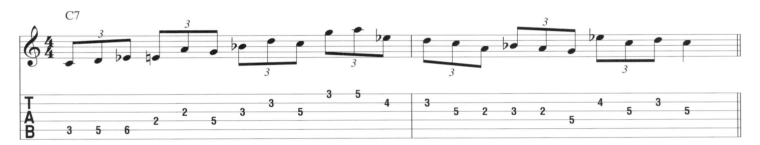

FIG. 6.37. Major Blues Septatonic Lick

Audio 44

And here's some similar material in constant sixteenths. This is the kind of phrasing that might be played over a jazz/funk groove.

FIG. 6.38. Constant Sixteenth Lick

- **Blues Arpeggio Resources.** Obviously, we can use typical four-note arpeggios in a blues, including the 1, 3, 5, ♭7, and also chord superimposition of an arpeggio based on the 3 of the chord (as discussed in an earlier chapter), which yields 3, 5, ♭7, 9.

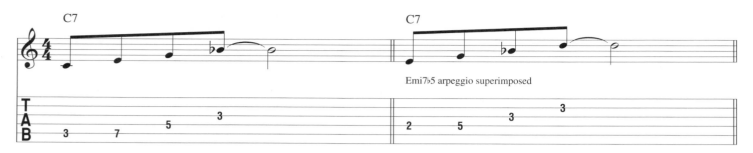

FIG. 6.39. Blues Arpeggios

These kinds of arpeggios are important and useful, but they are not particularly "bluesy" sounding. To inject the blues sound into an arpeggio passage, it helps to at least employ the ♭3 along with the other chord tones. The following "blues" arpeggios are a great way to incorporate a clearly bluesy sound into an arpeggio format.

- o **Movable major "blues" arpeggio:** ♭3, aka #9, usually played before the 3, ascending or descending

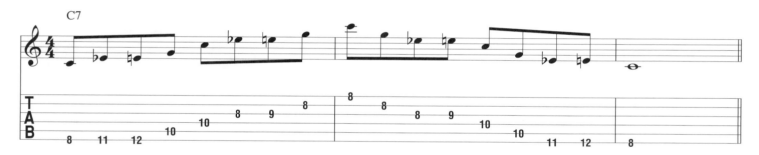

FIG. 6.40. Moveable "Blues" Arpeggio

- o **Descending Variation of "blues" arpeggio.** In this variation, in the descending form only, the notes ♭3 to ♮3 are replaced with ♭3 to 2 instead. It is typical and idiomatic for this to be used in descending form only (usually). This downward version of the arpeggio helps lead the ear downward.

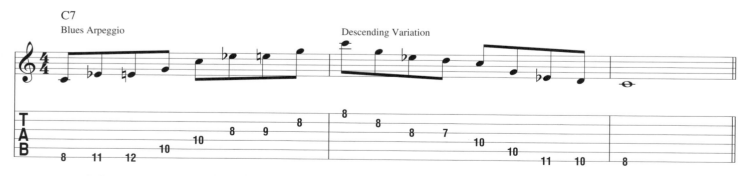

FIG. 6.41. Blues Arpeggio Ascending and then Descending

Here are a few practice strategies to help you gain familiarity with these sounds and fingerings:

- **Learn one two-octave movable form. Then move it to map out areas of activity for each chord all over the fretboard.** Figure 6.42 starts on the root of each chord, but you should also work out fingerings starting on the 3 and 5 and then shift them with this same approach.

FIG. 6.42. Practicing a Two-Octave Moveable Form

- Use exclusively one-octave fingerings corresponding to I7 IV7 and V7 (the chords in a basic three-chord blues). Apply these in real time over a blues form. Example in the key of C…

FIG. 6.43. Two-Octave Fingerings. Work out the arpeggios in one five- or six-fret area of the neck.

- Practice changing between the arpeggios with voice leading "on the fly," in tempo, between chord pairs.

- Break down your practice into all chord pairs that occur in the song form. In a basic three-chord blues in C, the chord pairs would be C7 to F7 (as below) then C7 to G7 and F7 to G7.

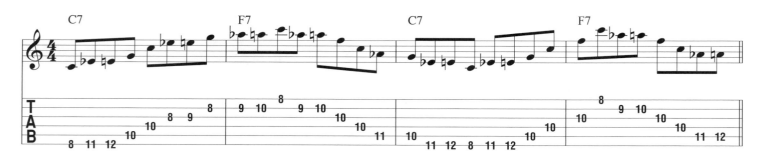

FIG. 6.44. Blues Arpeggio Chord Pairs Practice

- **Apply to a Blues Form.** After mastering the ability to transition with voice leading between the various chord pairs, apply this to an actual blues form. Below is the exercise applied to a simple three-chord blues in C. The notes in figure 6.45 represent only one of many possible ways of navigating the changes within the limited parameters of this exercise. Your goal is to become so familiar with the notes in these arpeggios and the form of the blues so that you can play a constant stream of notes drawn from them in real time and at steady tempo, and also "pre hear" and "pre-see" the way to voice lead into the next target tone by step. Remember, in the early phase of learning a new concept, it works best to intentionally limit your options in order to help you learn more effectively and thoroughly. Here, we are limited to using primarily stepwise transitions between arpeggios in a pre-defined "neighborhood" of the neck—ideally, an area you've been familiarizing yourself with during the previous preparation exercises.

Audio 45

FIG. 6.45. Blues Arpeggio Applied to Three-Chord Blues Exercise

This does not yet sound like a real improvisation of course; it's just an exercise to build control and familiarity. I encourage you to improvise these ideas against a blues backing track and begin to experiment with forming bits and pieces of this material into melodic phrases. The more you listen to great blues vocabulary, the more you will be able to hear and play musical melodies or musical lines based on these structures which, when "pre-heard" by you, will start to sound musical and organic.

- **Movable Chromatic Blues Gesture:** ♭3 ascending chromatically to 5. Our final resource is a completely chromatic idea which is very idiomatic and useful.

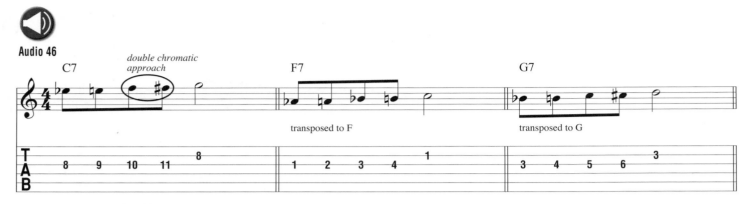

FIG. 6.46. Moveable Chromatic Blues Gesture

Getting these resources in your ear and under your fingers on the guitar, as with previously learned material, requires that you practice them in a variety of ways and with different fingerings which cover the entire fretboard.

Again, many of these devices are applied in the upcoming solo examples.

8. Hexatonics (Triad Pairing)

- An interesting "modern" sound can be achieved by using a technique called "triad pairing" to form six-note (hexatonic) scales extracted from typical seven- or eight-note scales.

The idea is to extract from a scale two diatonic triads that have no notes in common. The resulting six notes form a hexatonic scale.

Perhaps the most commonly used triad pair is the IV and V major triads in a major scale. In C major, those triads would be F and G.

That triad pair can be used to great effect on many of the chords diatonic to the key including the IImi7 chord (Dmi7) and the V7 (G7) and thus can be played over a IImi7 V7 progression.

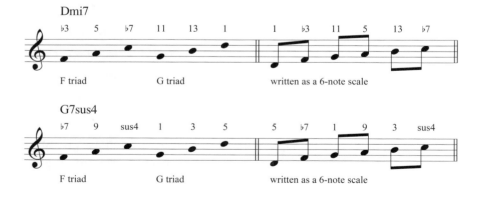

FIG. 6.47. Triad Pairs from C Major Forming Hexatonic Scale

Audio 47

We can use the resulting hexatonic scale as a resource for constant eighth-note lines. Here's one example.

FIG. 6.48. Hexatonic Scale from F and G Triad Pair Used for Constant Eighth-Note Line

We can also extract triad pairs from other scales. One cool sound to play over dominant chords comes from the altered scale. We can build a six-note scale from the ♭V and ♭VI major triads in the altered scale. Accessing the G altered dominant scale, we'd get the following:

FIG. 6.49. Hexatonic Scale from G Altered Scale

Audio 48

Here's a II V lick using F and G on the Dmi7 and D♭ and E♭ on the G7.

FIG. 6.50. II V Lick from G Altered Scale

There are many wonderful possibilities with this technique. I encourage you to investigate it further!

CHAPTER 7

Sample Solos
with Analysis

These solos use the concepts explored in chapters 1 to 6, including:

- Awareness of the guidelines for creating harmonically descriptive melodic lines listed in chapter 4
- Chord Scales
- Scale Patterns
- Arpeggios
- Superimposed Arpeggios
- 3 to 7/7 to 3 Voice Leading
- Digital Patterns
- Approach-Note Patterns
- Chromatic Connectors
- Bebop Scale Concept
- Blues Scales/Arpeggios and Idiomatic Licks

The solos are designed to illustrate these concepts and help you to improvise *harmonically expressive solos* over these progressions.

Indicated fingerings are optional; please feel free to experiment with others. But these fingerings do model the kinds of flexible fingerings that can help you transcend the limitations of position-based thinking. The note choices in the lines incorporate some motivic development and enough variety of shape and range to maintain interest in spite of lack of rhythmic variety.

Solos can be understood and analyzed "locally," in terms of four-note cells against the chord of the moment, and "globally" in terms of overall balance and direction.

Each solo is annotated. In chapter 8, I have included additional "rhythmicized" examples, altered to include rhythmic variety. Injecting rhythm into constant note-value improvisation chops is the next step towards fluency and musical application.

"JAZZ BLUES" SOLO

Four-note cells from various categories were used to build this solo, but the "whole/half crawl" (chromatic connector cell) in particular occurs frequently: three times, in measures 4, 6, and 10. Intentional repetition of one particular cell, while applying it to a variety of different chords, is an effective strategy for absorbing new vocabulary and also adds thematic development to a solo.

Fingerings are only suggestions, but these do model the use of the hand expansion/contraction technique (see chapter 5) to help facilitate position shifts up and down the neck, especially in the last few measures.

In addition to learning the solo, see if you can analyze/categorize the various four-note cells.

After learning the sample solo, try composing your own twelve-measure solo over the same chords. Try to make your solo carry on from the previous solo in a way that sounds related but not overly repetitive. Also, see if you can make use of one particular four-note cell at least three times on different chords as a kind of motif, as I did in the first chorus with the whole/half crawl cell.

One possible fingering is shown. In measures 10 to 12, notice that the fingering uses a slide and a lot of hand expansion/contraction to facilitate movement up the neck.

Audio 49–50

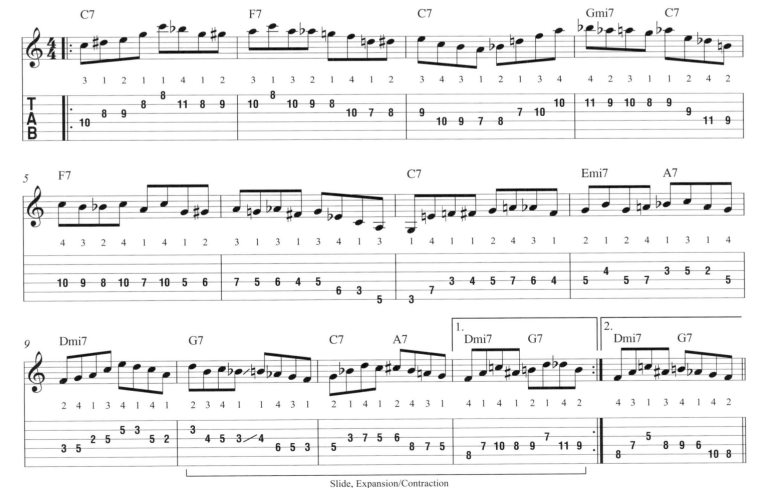

Slide, Expansion/Contraction

FIG. 7.1. "Jazz Blues" Solo

Compose Your Own Solo

Write your own constant eighth-note solo over these changes, using four-note cells.

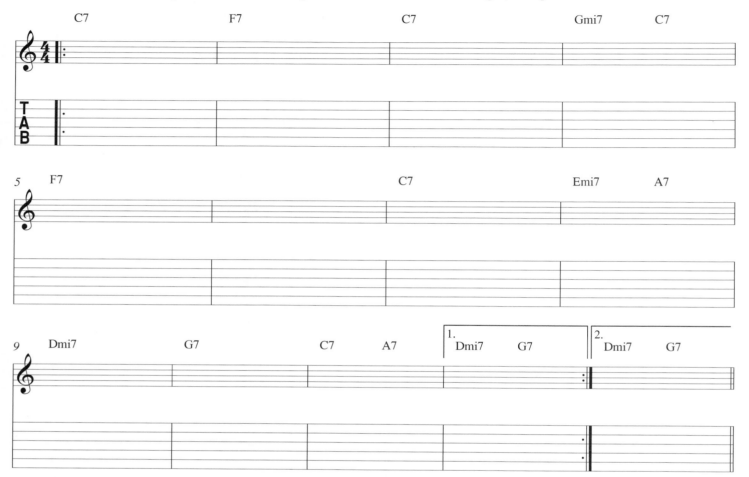

FIG. 7.2. Compose Your Own "Jazz Blues" Solo

"BIRD BLUES" SOLO

The next solo is over the harmonically embellished version of the blues made famous by Charles "Yardbird" Parker. This one purposely uses a limited number and type of four-note cells to demonstrate how much can be done with a limited amount of concepts. It is also annotated to show the different cells. After you learn it, there is some tutorial material to help you compose your own solo on a "Bird Blues."

Audio 51–52

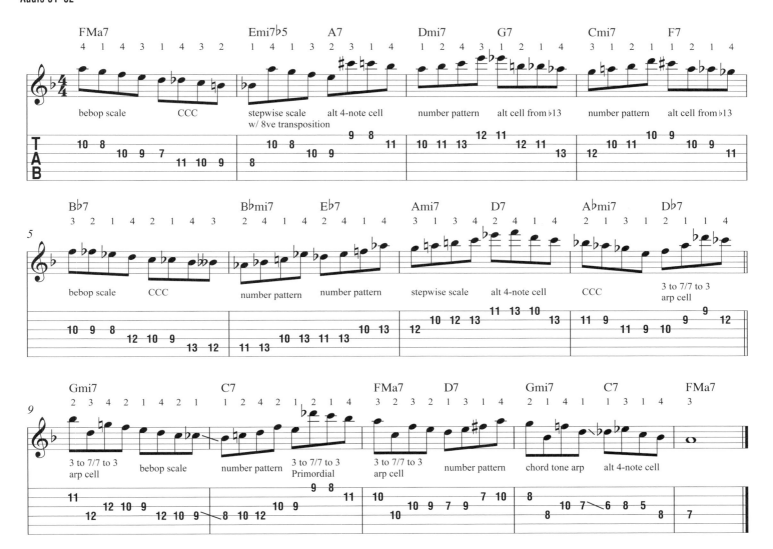

FIG. 7.3. "Bird Blues" Solo with Limited Four-Note Cells

Compose Your Own Solo

When you create your own "Bird Blues" solo, an effective strategy is to use a limited number of cells. To create variety, try choosing a mix of stepwise cells and arpeggio-based cells. I model the process below.

1. Scale-Based Cells

    - **Cell Concept 1** has scale-wise movement, including bebop chromatics. The variation has a ♭9 on a dominant 7, as in the primordial lick.

    - **Cell Concept 2** uses number pattern 1235, along with transpositions and inversions. Transpositions are shown starting on ♭7 and 3.

Audio 53

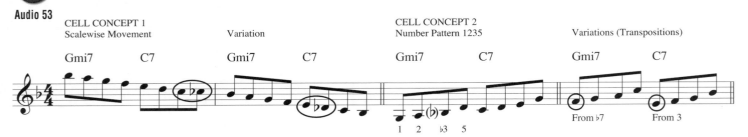

FIG. 7.4. Scale-Based Cells

2. Arpeggio-Based Cells

    - **Cell Concept 3** is based on 3 to 7/7 to 3 voice leading, with arpeggios and occasional chromatic approaches to help facilitate targeting the new chord. The note functions repeat in the new chord, but are varied with octave transpositions.

Audio 54

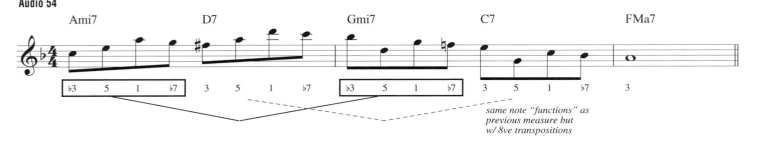

FIG. 7.5. Arpeggio-Based Cells

Audio 55

    - **Cell Concept 4.** Altered cells on dominant 7 chords are varied using at least two altered notes: ♭9, ♯9, ♯11, ♭13.

FIG. 7.6. Altered Cells

- In the first excerpt, without CCC, the cell ends on A as the target note. The following variation uses CCC, which engineers a stepwise arrival to a chord tone on B♭, the ♭5 of Emi7♭5, as my target note. In both cases, the notes work against the chord of the moment, but CCC gives the flexibility to target either one.

Audio 56

FIG. 7.7. Cell Using CCC to Arrive on a Chord Tone

Now you try! Compose a "Bird Blues," constant eighth-note solo with a limited number of four-note cells.

- **Step 1:** Pick five of your favorite four-note cells and write them below as they would apply to C7. Try for a mix of vertical (arpeggio based) and horizontal (scalar) types.

FIG. 7.8. Write Your Own Four-Note Cells

- **Step 2:** Pick one of your chosen four-note cells, transpose it to fit the first chord, and begin! As you go you'll need to transpose your cells, written above in relation to C7, to fit the chord of the moment. For example, if one of your cells is 1, 2, 3, 5, the note against C7 would be C, D, E, G but the notes against FMa7 would be F, G, A, C, etc.

Remember the guidelines:

- Set chord tones and available tensions on downbeats (exception is "blues" licks).

- Move by step at point of chord change (exception, you can leap into chord tones and available tensions, but do so sparingly).

- Altered tensions (♭9, #9, ♭13) work on dominant 7 chords only.

- Go for an overall balance of vertical and horizontal movement in the solo.

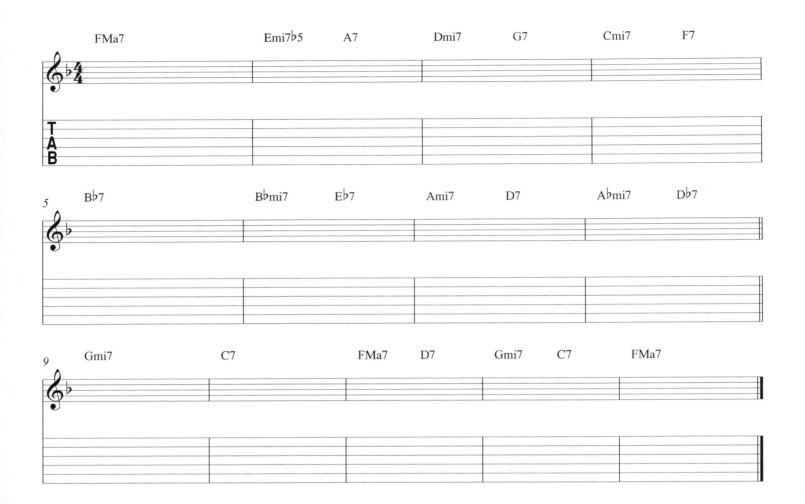

FIG. 7.9. Compose Your Own "Bird Blues" Solo

"RHYTHM CHANGES" SOLOS

Here's a solo on the "I Got Rhythm" chord changes ("Rhythm Changes," for short). For the most part, it only uses five four-note cell concepts:

- **Bebop Scale.** Extra half step between two "available" notes.

- **CCC.** Extra half step as needed to all for chromatic approach by step.

- **Altered Scale.** On dominant 7 chords only, cells using any combination of notes from the altered scale: ♭9, ♯9, ♭13, ♯11.

- **Arpeggio.** Exclusively notes of the chord or a chord superimposition.

- **2+1/1+2.** Either two chromatics from above/one from below or one chromatic from above/two from below.

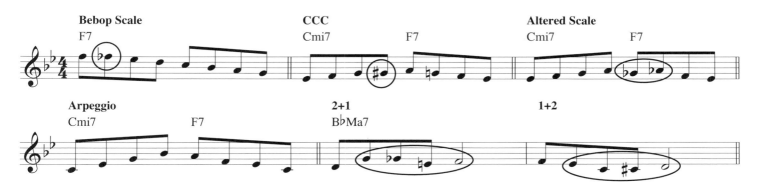

FIG. 7.10. Cells Used in the "Rhythm Changes" Solo

So far, provided fingerings have utilized shifts and hand compression/expansion to facilitate movement around the neck. These are not intended as the only—or even the best—way to locate and finger the notes. They are examples to encourage you to think creatively about fingerings and note location.

Going forward, I'll include tablature, but am purposely leaving out my own fingerings so that you can have the experience of problem-solving the suggested note locations with your own fingerings. Dealing with "fingering puzzles," once you're aware of more options, is the next step in developing your own fingering choices. Memorizing a lot of set fingerings is not the goal. Rather, learning to be able to think of and execute multiple options is the skill guitarists need to develop to become fluent improvisers. We need to be able to consider alternatives. What will make this passage sound more musically effective? More legato? More percussive? Easier to play at faster tempos?

Audio 57–58

Come up with your own fingerings and note locations, and you'll gain greater mastery.

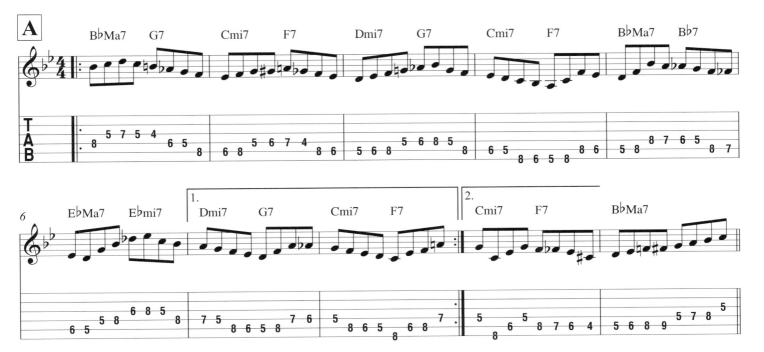

FIG. 7.11. "Rhythm Changes" Solo

Compose Your Own Solo

Compose your own "Rhythm Changes" solo, using the techniques we discussed.

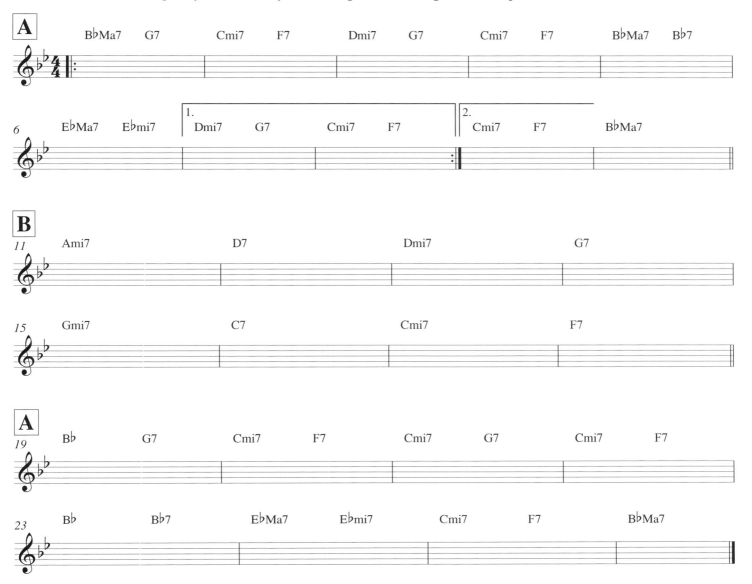

FIG. 7.12. Compose Your Own Solo on "Rhythm Changes"

"COLTRANE CHANGES" SOLO

Audio 59–60

The following solo utilizes a variety of four-note cells, including some frequently used by Coltrane himself when he played over these types of harmonic patterns.

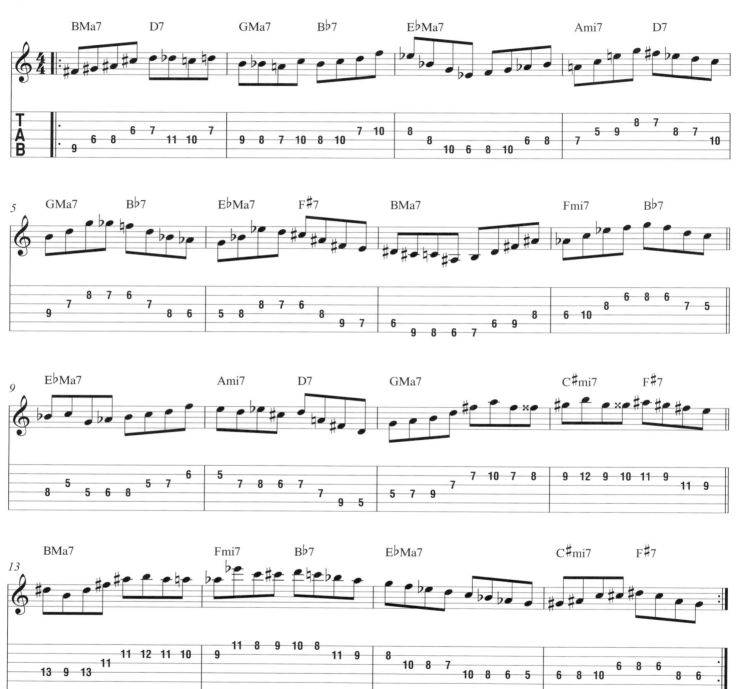

FIG. 7.13. "Coltrane Changes" Solo

Compose Your Own Solo

Compose your own solo on "Coltrane Changes."

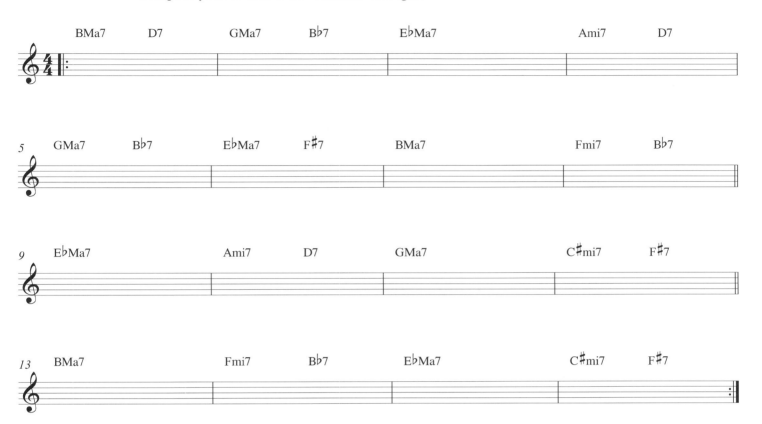

FIG. 7.14. Compose Your Own Solo on "Coltrane Changes"

CHAPTER 8

Strategies for Rhythmic Variation

The concept of soloing with constant note values is a means to an end. It makes you have to deal with the harmony and master it. But once you have some skill, you should also work on soloing outside the restrictions of constant note value exercises by adding rhythmic variation to your ideas.

Here are a few strategies for doing that:

1. Use melodic motives (either from the song melody or ones that you create) that have inherent rhythmic variation, and manipulate and transpose them through the chord changes to express the harmony.

2. Take constant eighth-note ideas, and edit them into syncopated passages.

3. Used "tied" rhythms and rests to create syncopations.

4. Use triplets and triplet-derived rhythms and other tuplet groupings, such as quintuplets and septuplets.

Next are three solos based on progressions in chapter 7, with some of these strategies applied.

"COLTRANE CHANGES" SOLO WITH VARIED RHYTHMS

Following is a "Coltrane Changes" composition that uses many four-note cells transformed with rhythmic variety. See if you can analyze the various melodic devices and target notes. The harmony is still expressed, though more liberally and with some rhythmic displacement.

FIG. 8.1. "Coltrane Changes" Solo with Varied Rhythms

Audio 62–63

"REBOP" SOLO WITH VARIED RHYTHMS

Here is a "Rhythm Changes" composition that uses many four-note cells transformed rhythmically. Can you recognize the cell types and target notes? The harmony is still expressed but with rhythmic variety and displacement integrated into the lines.

FIG. 8.2. "Rebop" Solo with Varied Rhythms

"BIRD BLUES" SOLO WITH VARIED RHYTHMS—AND SOME CLOSING THOUGHTS

This is a completely improvised solo that, except for one muffled note, has not been fixed or edited. In contrast, all of the constant eighth-note solos in this book *are* carefully curated and edited to illustrate particular concepts. I'm including this solo to help you see the difference between the two approaches. One is for practice and skill building; the other is for in-the-moment creative expression. Hopefully, hearing and analyzing this solo will help you make the connection between study/ practice and "real world" playing.

Studying and learning to play and improvise constant note value solos is of tremendous benefit in helping you *build a foundation* from which to launch your improvisations. But when you are actually playing with a band, the idea is to tell— or some would say, find—a story and have an interaction with the band. You are *all* finding the story together. It's just that the soloist is usually taking the lead role most of the time. For the music to have life, you actually don't want to plan out everything that you are going to play but rather rely on your training to help you communicate in the moment.

Another analogy is sports. Who would want to watch a sporting event in which everything was pre-planned? A sporting event is meant to be surprising, while at the same time, the players are operating within the structure and rules of the game they are playing. It's that great balance of training, structure, and freedom of expression that makes for compelling creative experiences.

Improvising is really about following what your inner musical ear is generating, in the moment, in response to all the other elements that are happening simultaneously.

These include:

- The time feel and notes being generated by yourself and the other members of the band.

- The totality of sound being generated by your instruments in the acoustical environment you are playing in.

- The audience.

- Your musical imagination and technique.

This solo is not heavily interactive because I was still trying to generate a lot of eighth notes for pedagogical reasons, but what is played is certainly influenced by what the rhythm section players are generating.

Analyzing the solo reveals that it's a blend of some concepts from the book and other concepts not yet discussed in this book, but which are techniques that round out an improvisation and help it come to life.

Concepts from the book used in this improvised solo include:

- Balance of horizontal and vertical in melodic line
- Placement of chord tones/available tensions on downbeats, the vast majority of the time
- Motivic manipulation (sequencing)
- Arpeggio cells
- Scale cells
- Altered cells
- Movement by step at point of chord change (voice leading)
- Various forms of blues scales and arpeggios
- Approach-tone patterns (multiple)
- Bebop scale
- Chromatic cells and gestures

Concepts *beyond the focus of this book* that are used in this improvised solo include:

- Reharmonization "on the fly"
- Rhythmic displacement
- Rhythmic variety (triplets/sixteenths)
- Syncopation/anticipation/delay
- Motivic manipulation (inversion, retrograde and transpositions of them)
- Leaving space/using long duration notes, to help define phrases and let the music breathe
- Points in time where phrasing is more important than specific notes and where phrasing is the *primary* element creating interest and forward motion

One value of learning to categorize and analyze music is that it helps you ultimately use for yourself, the elements you like.

I have annotated only a few of the more obvious elements listed above. I recommend that you study and analyze this solo further and extract the elements you like for your own practice and use. And of course, keep doing this with any improvised solo you want to study.

For help with the "beyond-the-scope-of-this-book" elements mentioned above, there are many resources out there including private instruction with a teacher and a multitude of books and lessons on the art of improvisation. But don't forget that perhaps the most direct and beneficial approach of all is to transcribe, analyze, learn to play, and extract concepts and elements from solos by improvisers who inspire you.

Improvised "Bird Blues" Solo
with Varied Rhythms

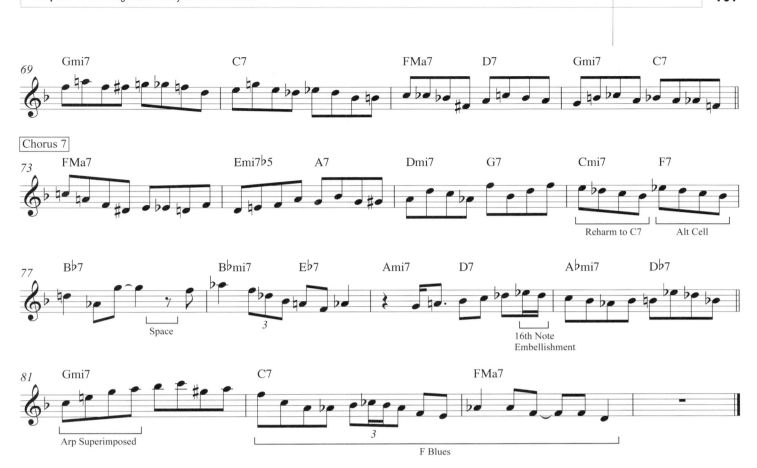

FIG. 8.3. "Bird Blues" Improvisation. Backing track audio courtesy of Martin Gioani.

ABOUT THE AUTHOR

Photo by Marv Goldschmitt

Guitarist, composer, educator Steven Kirby ("a guitarist of rippling technique and a poetic mind"- *DownBeat*) is known for performing exciting, melodic, lyrical and expressive jazz as well as performing in other contemporary styles. He has appeared on multiple recordings including three as a leader: *Point of Balance* and *North Light* (Challenge Records), and *Illuminations* (WCS Records). *Illuminations* was a *DownBeat* magazine's Editors' Pick and was included on the Grammy Nominations long list in four categories. He has performed and/or recorded with many of today's most respected contemporary musicians including Chris Potter, Mike Manieri (Steps Ahead), Joe Lovano, Harvie S, Steve Hunt, Allan Holdsworth, and others. He has toured in the U.S., Canada, Caribbean, Europe, China, and Africa.

Kirby's music has been played on over 100 radio stations in the U.S. and internationally including features on NPR's *Here and Now*, *Jazz with Bob Parlocha*, and *Eric in the Evening*.

His jazz compositions have won awards in the International Songwriting Competition, the *Billboard* Song Contest, and *DownBeat*. He is a graduate of Berklee College of Music and has a master's degree in jazz composition and arranging from the University of Massachusetts (Amherst).

Kirby has published articles in *Guitar Player Magazine*, *Jazz Improv Magazine*, and others. He is currently an associate professor (Harmony Dept.) at Berklee College of Music and teaches as a visiting professor at Wellesley College.

From Selected Reviews:

"Kirby's music manifests the truth that jazz is an art built on growth and renewal... an extraordinarily pleasing and diverse album." (*All About Jazz*)

"Steven Kirby, guitarist of rippling technique and a poetic mind, has developed a modern jazz guitar style that bridges the angular lyricism of Pat Metheny and the painterly asceticism of Jim Hall." (*DownBeat*)

"Meticulously played, elegantly produced ... Kirby has a serious command of the guitar." (*New England Performer*)

"Steven Kirby's *Illuminations* features deep beauty and folkloric elegance while also an album that doesn't lose sight of Kirby's jazz roots and penchant for more incendiary playing . . . *Illuminations* represents Kirby's biggest leap forward yet—as a writer but, equally, as a guitarist who leans towards inimitable lyricism yet also possesses the chops to burn brightly as the music demands it." (John Kelman, music journalist and noted author of multiple ECM records liner notes)